D1491020

A Woman
by God's
Grace

The Best in Wholesome Reading
CHOICE BOOKS Dept. 243
11923 Lee Highway
Fairfax, VA 22030
We Welcome Your Response

A Woman

by God's

Grace

"her candle goeth not out
by night." Proverbs 31:18

A sequel to "A Woman for God's Glory

Anna Mary Byler

Distributed by Choice Books of Northern Virginia
11923 Lee Highway, Fairfax, VA 22030 (703) 830-2800

Copies may also be obtained from the author at:
Route 1, Box 630, Stuarts Draft, VA 24477

ISBN: 0-940883-04-X

Attempt has been made to secure permission for the use of all copyrighted material. We have reason to believe some of these poems were written in the early nineteenth century and, therefore, are in public domain. We welcome any information which will help rectify any needed reference or credits. It will be our privilege to make any adjustments in future editions.

Unless otherwise stated, all Scripture quotations are taken from the King James Version.

Printed by Campbell Copy Center
Harrisonburg, Virginia

Table of Contents

In an ideal Christian family . . .

C hrist is given first place.
H appiness prevails.
R ejoicing is heard instead of complaints.
I nterruptions don't destroy family peace.
S torms strengthen a family's love.
T ears and disappointments are shared openly.
I n difficult times, everyone is drawn closer to God.
A visitor always feels welcome.
N eeds of others come before our own needs.

F ussing is not heard.
A time of separation does not sever strong family ties.
M oney is kept in proper perspective.
I nterest is shown equally in every family member.
L ove covers the faults in others.
Y oung people respect and obey their parents.

—Shirley Byler
February 4, 1992

I Need You, God

Dear God, I do not want to know
What things there are in store
But I implore your help to live
And to accomplish more.
Your hand alone can lead me through
The darkness of the night
And bless me with encouragement
To keep on doing right.
I try to be prepared each day
To take my life in stride . . .
But I need grace to guide my steps
And never leave your side.
Almighty God, in every thought
I most sincerely pray
For just enough assistance now
That I may never stray.
Be with me every morning when
The sky is gray or blue
And let me find the stars at night
That light the way to you.

Courtesy of Baxter Lane Company, Armarillo, TX, 1975.
Used by permission.

Writer's Acknowledgments

*"Now therefore let it please thee to bless the [writing] of thy servant
. . . for thou blessest, O Lord, and it shall be blessed for ever"*
(I Chronicles 17:27).

I am deeply indebted . . .

. . . To my loving heavenly Father . . . who "called me by his grace," Galatians 1:15. Grace is described as love that stoops. I have experienced God's mercy as He stooped to extend His wonderful grace to me. For that reason I am what I am.

. . . To Bennie, my dear husband, who took time from his busy schedule once again to read my scrawls. I desire this book to be an extension and reflection of his ministry.

. . . To my loving children:
Sue, for her encouragement, help in typing, and financial assistance.

Sharon, for giving her talent in doing the calligraphy on the cover.

Shirley, for designing the cover, and for her untiring help and encouragement in arranging the entire book.

Steve and Rosa and my precious grandchildren, Douglas and Margaret, who were willing to leave the comforts of family, church, and answered God's call to pioneer an Anabaptist church in Ireland, therefore extending our family's horizon.

. . . To Anita Yoder for cheerfully giving many hours to type the manuscript.

. . . To Dan Yoder, Ervin Hershberger, Linda Rose, David and Paul Miller, Lavina Gingerich, and others who proofread the manuscript.

. . . To those of Pilgrim Church who permitted me to use some illustrations and experiences and to those who encouraged and prayed.

I, as a writer, acknowledge my humanity. I have meant to be fair, accurate, and truthful in all my writing. I am also aware of my unworthiness, but I humbly believe I also know something about the worthiness of an all-sufficient Saviour and of the wonderful grace of God that is worthy of all glory and praise.

It was the writer of Proverbs who acknowledged that it is the godly woman's candle that gives light during the night. Even if my candle is but a small light, it is my prayer that there may be those who can light their candle by its flame.

May this feeble attempt articulate the powerful truths of the Scripture and give insight and encouragement to all who desire to become *A Woman by God's Grace*.

"That they may know that this is thy hand; that thou, Lord, hast done it" (Psalm 109:27).

Introduction

Grace is defined as the unmerited, undeserved favor with God. This is the exchange that God gives when self ends at Calvary. The wonderful grace of God transforms a sinner into a saint. It makes duty a delight. Titus 2:11 reminds us that "the grace of God . . . hath appeared to all [people]."

It is this grace that makes it possible that our *hearts* can be His *prepared* dwelling place, *perfect and purposeful*. It is the grace of God that gives daily strength through *daily manna* whereby we can live victoriously. The family now can experience worship each day, which reminds each one of whose we are and whom we serve. The husband can then be an *umbrella of security* for his wife and children. The wife can become *a true counterpart*, and the children can grow up to be a *strength rather than a stress*. The grace of God directs the husband so he can *follow the leader*, Christ. The whole family knows where they are going because heaven is their goal. The grace of God is that *hedge of protection* as the family meets God's commandments and requirements. *Termites* may try to invade the home, but they are conquered before crucial damage is done.

It is the grace of God that points to God's truth for answers when problems arise. Therefore, we are able to *find the solution* for our problems because we are not satisfied to go around in circles. His grace enables us to mature and become more Christlike.

The grace of God does not allow us to *live in the basement* of our spiritual life, but instead, we will feed our spiritual life so we will become a complete person in Christ. In such a condition, we are able to love our spouse and children *without a "net,"* because of our concern that each one grows to become all God has planned for their lives.

God's grace discerns what is *noble* and what pleases God rather than desiring to be *noticed.* Because we now live unto God, we find His yoke easy and His burden light. Therefore, we are *prepared for the rainy days* that are sure to come. We will not lament the fact that our life is fearful and unfulfilled.

God's grace makes it a privilege to *walk the chalk line* of God's truth, since it is the truth that makes us free. We count it a blessing to *gather up the fragments,* rather than desiring that all our belongings must be either new or the best in quality.

By God's grace we enjoy our children when they demand all of our attention with little or no appreciation. Later in life we can *reflect back* with fond memories and few regrets. Then, as they grow older, our children will still need us as mothers, but not to the extent as when they were younger. Meanwhile, we will find *joy in housecleaning.* Although we are *working ourselves out of a job,* by His grace, we will find continual fulfillment in following the Shepherd, knowing there are other blessings in store for the faithful woman.

Since her candle "goeth not out by night," her influence continues on even after she has passed from this life. It is then the wonderful grace of God that will usher the faithful woman into His presence, because she was *A Woman for God's Glory, A Woman by God's Grace.*

Preface

Each time a baby girl is born, a lifetime of choices is begun. She will grow either to become like the submitted and beautiful Bride of Christ or like the proud and rebellious harlot of Babylon. In all of God's creation, what is more lovely and attractive than the woman who permits the grace of God to radiate through her life the purity, the humility, the softness that God intended for the female gender? On the contrary, what is less attractive or desirable than a dirty, loudmouthed, selfish, and bossy woman?

As we consider the great contrast between these two, what is it that determines which description best fits your life? Is it not, in essence, your response to the grace of God?

The Bible contains the mind of God and reveals His marvelous love and grace for all humanity. To the degree that any individual accepts the truth of God's Word in a personal, life-changing way, to that degree will that person's life radiate the love and beauty that comes from God.

The feminist movement of our generation has been preaching a different message: the message that women must become more assertive, independent, demanding their rights. This doctrine is totally self-seeking, rejecting the plan and purpose of God. And what are the results? We are witnessing a society that is crumbling at the very foundation, seemingly spinning totally out of control.

Will we come back to God's way before it is too late?

We may not be able to control or decide what others will do, but each one of us decides what course we will take. This is not a once-for-all choice, but many small decisions that are made throughout each day.

That's what this book is all about—reminding and encouraging you, the reader, to set the right priorities and to make wise choices in your everyday life and responsibilities. May the Spirit of God warm your heart and draw you to Himself, that His grace may permeate your life and make your life beautiful for Him!

Dan and Barbara Yoder

William Carey's lifelong motto:
 Expect great things from a great God
 Attempt great things for a great God.

O For A Heart

O for a heart that is whiter than snow!
Kept, ever kept, 'neath the life-giving flow;
Cleansed from all passion, self-seeking and pride,
Washed in the fountain of Calvary's tide.

O for a heart that is whiter than snow!
Calm in the peace He loves to bestow;
Daily refreshed by the heavenly dews,
Ready for service whene'er He shall choose.

O for a heart that is whiter than snow!
With the pure flame of the Spirit aglow;
Filled with a love that is true and sincere,
Love that is able to banish all fear.

O for a heart that is whiter than snow!
Then in His grace and His knowledge to grow;
Growing like Him who my pattern shall be,
Till in His beauty my King I shall see.

O for a heart that is whiter than snow!
Saviour divine, to whom else can I go?
Thou who didst die, loving me so,
Give me a heart that is whiter than snow.

—E. E. Hewitt

Used by permission. Aaron Z. Weaver, 1972

1

A Heart—Prepared, Perfect, Purposeful

In the seventeenth century, Charles Wesley was inspired to pen the words, "O for a heart to praise my God, a heart from sin set free, a heart that is sprinkled with the blood, so freely shed for me." The illustrates a *prepared heart*, one that is God's dwelling place.

"A Heart resigned, submissive, meek, my dear Redeemer's throne, where only Christ is heard to speak, where Jesus reigns alone. A heart in every thought renewed and full of love divine, perfect and right and pure, and good, a copy, Lord, of Thine. An humble, lowly, contrite heart, believing, true, and clean, which neither life nor death can part from Him that dwells within." This describes a *perfect heart*.

"Thy nature gracious Lord impart, come quickly from above—write Thy new name upon my heart, Thy new best name of love." This defines a *prepared, perfect, and purposeful heart*, willing to serve God wholeheartedly.

Down through the ages, God spoke and worked through His people. Only those who had prepared their hearts to do God's bidding followed Him closely and carefully. God's eyes "run to and fro throughout the whole earth, to shew himself strong in the behalf of them whose heart is perfect toward him" (II Chronicles 16:9a). According to I Chronicles 28:9, 10, we are to "know . . . the

God of thy father, and serve him with a perfect heart and a willing mind: for the Lord searcheth all hearts . . . if thou seek him, he will be found of thee . . . take heed [be very careful] . . . be strong, and do it."

Abraham had a prepared heart. In Genesis 17:1, God said, "Walk before me, and be thou perfect." It is interesting to note that Abraham is the first to be called out by God from the generation of Shem, Noah's son. In Genesis 12:2, God promised Abraham, "I will make of thee a great nation." Abraham obeyed and followed God precisely. God looked into Abraham's heart and saw a prepared heart, a heart that desired to please Him. When God spoke, Abraham obeyed. Obedience to God is the first ingredient of a prepared heart. Obedience must be carried out to the finest detail, because God does not overlook any sin when He seeks for a prepared heart as His tabernacle.

Joseph is an outstanding example of one who had a perfect heart. When he was a small boy, his mother died, leaving him without a mother's instruction and encouragement. Because he grew up being his father's favorite, he was often mistreated by his brothers. At seventeen, he was sold as a slave into Egypt. He was misrepresented, falsely accused, rejected, and even forgotten in prison. All the time God was testing him, and he proved faithful.

Early in life Joseph's heart was prepared for God's dwelling place. God was preparing him for the promotion of being next to Pharaoh. After these many trials in his life, Joseph was brought from prison to Pharaoh to interpret his dreams. Joseph was quick to recognize God. "It is not in me: God shall give Pharaoh an answer of peace" (Genesis 41:16). This was the secret of Joseph's dedicated life. It is still the same today. If our heart is God's dwelling place and is perfect before God, we too will be quick to acknowledge it is God and not of man. No wonder Pharaoh said, "Can we find such a one as this is, a man in whom the spirit of God is?" (Genesis 41:38).

Joseph's life speaks of practical wisdom. He had conviction that did not allow him to commit sin, even though it would cost him years in prison. Instead, he was willing to be falsely accused, leaving his coat in Potiphar's wife's hand. Daniel is another example of one who prepared his heart and was perfect before God. Therefore, he purposed in his heart to serve God only. Daniel was taken captive as a young man. He met the demands of the king, who was looking for young men who would benefit his kingdom. Even though the king had rules, "Daniel purposed in his heart that he would not defile himself" (Daniel 1:8).

God blessed Daniel as God still blesses people today when they are willing to be counted for Him. In spite of the fact that Daniel was miles from his home and his family, he still "purposed in his heart." Because of his obedience, God gave him knowledge and skill in all learning and wisdom.

When the king had a dream, he noted that Daniel could interpret it (Daniel 2:19). The secret of Daniel's success was "Then Daniel blessed the God of heaven. . . . Blessed be the name of God forever and ever" (Daniel 2:19b, 20). Later Daniel was called by the king again to interpret, and immediately Daniel's reply was, "But there is a God in heaven that revealeth secrets and maketh known . . ." (Daniel 2:28a). Much was accomplished because Daniel had prepared his heart and was perfect before God. Therefore, he had a purpose to serve God wholeheartedly. Obedience is the mark of such a heart. To God, it is so important that it ranks above all other obedience. We must obey God rather than men. We would be following the best of God's men if we emulate Daniel, Joseph, or Abraham in their example of trust and obedience.

Next to obedience is the desire to please our Maker. When the desire to please is in our hearts, it is accompanied by godly fear. In Exodus 23:27, God says, "I will send my fear before thee. . . ." God promises protection from the enemy that would hinder our hearts from being perfect before Him. Godly fear must fill our hearts. Proverbs 14:26 says, "In the fear of the Lord is strong confidence." In Proverbs 1:7 we read, "The fear of the Lord is beginning of knowledge." When God's fear is part of our heart, we can "be holy for [God is] holy" (Leviticus 11:44).

We must see and know the exceeding sinfulness of sin (Romans 7:13) in order to get a glimpse of God's holiness. In God's sight, sin is sin; there are none who are less sinful, because it cost God His beloved Son to give His life for our redemption, for all sin. Solomon tells us it is "the little foxes that spoil the vines" (Song of Solomon 2:15). So it is in our lives. It is those "little things" we sometimes give different names, such as attitudes, personalities, faults, or weaknesses. These are all sins that hinder our hearts from being pure and perfect tabernacles. All must be confessed and repented of in order for God to dwell there.

Selfishness and pride are continually in combat with my desire to be Christlike; therefore, I must die daily (Galatians 2:20).

Careless speech is a real hindrance. Our words must be "Yea, yea; Nay; nay: for whatsoever is more than these cometh of evil" (Matthew 5:37). "Let no corrupt communication proceed out of your mouth" (Ephesians 4:29). "How forcible are right words! but what doth your arguing reprove?" (Job 6:25). "Death and life are in the power of the tongue" (Proverbs 18:21). We must "speak the truth in love" (Ephesians 4:15). Like Job we must pray that God will "teach me, and I will hold my tongue" (Job 6:24). Only God can control and tame that "unruly evil, full of deadly poison" (James 3:8).

Satan uses partial truth as another means of defeating God's prepared dwelling place. "A double minded man is unstable in all his ways" (James 1:8). It is human and so easy to agree with everyone and yet not know where we stand. God expects us to be those who "... continue in my [Jesus'] word, then are ye my disciples indeed; And ye shall know the truth, and the truth shall make you free" (John 8:31, 32). God sees right through the dual lifestyle, deep into the heart. There is nothing we can hide from God; therefore, we must bring into captivity every thought or imagination to the obedience of Christ (II Corinthians 10:5). It is so important to "keep [our hearts] with all diligence; for out of it are the issues of life" (Proverbs 4:23). Another hindrance to a prepared heart is neglecting Bible study and prayer. We must drink deeply and daily to be able to live victoriously. "Thy word have I hid in mine heart, and I might not sin against thee" (Psalm 119:11). "O how love I thy law! it is my meditation all the day" (Psalm 119:97). It is evident whether we love or tolerate God's Word. In the same measure, we will experience victory or defeat. The saying is very true, "What we feed grows!" So in our devotion to God, when we feed on God's Word, we will grow closer to God. When we feed on trash, that is what will spill out at an unguard moment. God is able to fill our hearts so full of Himself that nothing can come forth but love. An old illustration is descriptive here: "A cup brimful of sweet water cannot spill one drop of bitter water however suddenly jolted." A person must "study to shew thyself approved unto God, a workman that needeth not to be ashamed, rightly dividing the word of truth" (II Timothy 2:15). Our conviction is no deeper than our depth of God's Word; therefore, it behooves all of us to diligently study to know God's will and His way. Conviction is based on God's Word; preference, on human reasoning. There is real need to keep a proper balance to maintain conviction and biblical practices.

Materialism robs God of being first in our heart; therefore, trust and faith in God is choked out. We become insensitive to God's "still small voice" (I Kings

19:12). God placed us in the world, but we are not to be of the world (John 17:16).

In order for us to be light and salt (Matthew 5:13, 16), our hearts must be God's prepared dwelling. Then His love can radiate through our lives to bring glory to God. "Set your affection on things above" (Colossians 3:2). "Seek ye first the kingdom of God, and his righteousness" (Matthew 6:33). God promises that all our needs shall be supplied. The songwriter says it well: "When we get a glimpse of God, "the things of earth will grow strangely dim, in the light of His glory and grace."

Jealousy and envy, even though they may be unnoticed by people, keep our hearts from being God's tabernacles. The antidote for envy is praying for the one who succeeds, rejoicing when he rejoices, and encouraging him to be all God wants him to be. All too often, we desire to be where someone else is and fail in being a prepared heart for God.

God always has answers for our every need. "Cast away from you all your transgressions, whereby ye have transgressed; and make you a new heart and new spirit" (Ezekiel 18:31). God asks us to make a complete change in our lives, then our hearts will be new. "I will give them one heart, and I will put a new spirit within you; and I [God] will take the stony heart out of their flesh, and will give them a [pliable] heart of flesh" (Ezekiel 11:19, 20). Then God's plea will be granted, "O that there were such a heart in them, that they would fear me and keep all my commandments always" (Deuteronomy 5:29). God is still looking for a dwelling place in the tabernacle of our hearts. When we meet God's conditions, He says, "And there will I meet with thee, and I will commune with thee" (Exodus 25:22a) in the heart that is prepared, perfect, and purposeful.

Early in his life D. L. Moody made an important discovery to success. He spread out his petitions before God and then said, "Thy will be done." It was the sweetest lesson he had learned in the school of obedience: to let God lead and choose for him.

My Bible

When I am tired, the Bible is my bed;
   Or in the dark, the Bible is my light.
When I am hungry, it is vital bread;
   Or fearful, it is armor for the fight.
When I am sick, 'tis healing medicine;
Or lonely, thronging friends I find therein.

If I would work, the Bible is my tool;
   Or play, it is a harp of happy sound.
If I am ignorant, it is my school;
   If I am sinking, it is solid ground.
If I am cold, the Bible is my fire;
And it is wings, if boldly I aspire.

Should I be lost, the Bible is my guide;
   Or naked, it is raiment rich and warm.
Am I imprisoned, it ranges wide;
   Or tempest-tossed, a shelter from the storm.
Would I adventure, 'tis a gallant sea;
Or would I rest, it is a flowerly lea.

Does gloom oppress? The Bible is a sun.
   Or ugliness? It is a garden fair.
Am I athirst? How cool its currents run!
   Or stifled? What a vivifying air!
Since thus thou givest of thyself to me,
How should I give myself, great Book, to thee!

Courtesy of Back to the Bible Broadcast, Lincoln, NE.
Used by permission.

2

Daily Manna

Imagine with me, for a few minutes, that we are two little children who left Egypt with the Israelites that night. We remember hearing the cries of the Egyptians as they found their firstborn dead. We hear our parents say, "Hurry, we must go!"

* * *

We are among the multitude that walked through the Red Sea on dry ground and we hear our great leader, Moses, sing the song of victory when all the Egyptians drowned in the sea.

* * *

We hear our parents talk of all the wonderful works of God. We all bow our heads with theirs in reverence and thanksgiving for His great deliverance.

* * *

As we travel, it gets tiresome and we are weary. The animals are becoming unruly. The babies become fussy, but even so, we must stay on the move.

The day wears on; the sun becomes more pressing and we can hardly keep up with the family. Then we hear our two-year-old say, "Mama, I want to go home. I want my bed." She cheerfully explains that we are going to a new home where we will have plenty of honey and milk, and where everything will be pleasant.

* * *

All throughout the camp, people are asking for water. The animals are becoming thirsty, too. In a moment of impatience, someone is heard accusing Moses for bringing the whole group out into the desert to die of thirst. We become fearful! Will we die for lack of water? But, as before, Moses calls upon God. We catch a glimpse of him on his knees with his hands covering his face, pleading to the great God.

God answered his prayer and soon everyone and every animal had refreshing water to their fill. We hear people rejoicing, but not for long. Fear grips our hearts as we hear grown-ups complaining about the low supply of food. Did we hear correctly? Do they really want to go back to Egypt again? Don't they remember the lashings for not working hard enough?

We look at each other. "Poor Moses," I whisper to my friend, "what is he going to do now?"

Sure enough, we see him with his face buried in his hands, down on his knees. He looks like he is crying. We feel like crying too! Don't these grown-ups know how distressing they make it sound for little ears?

Once again Moses, now with a shining face, rebukes the complaining people, yet lovingly assures them that God is going to supply their need (Exodus 16:12b) "...and in the morning ... ye shall know that I am the Lord your God."

Manna, fresh manna, the next morning! It is God's miraculous provision for His children.

For forty years God supplied manna, fresh manna, for His children. But like all of God's blessings, there were requirements to meet.

They were to gather manna every morning, but if someone tried to gather for the next day, "it bred worms, and stank" (Exodus 16:20b).

We, like the Israelites, have left our Egypt. We are on our way to our heavenly Canaan. Far too often, we complain and murmur, but instead, we should plead to

God for forgiveness.

Every morning we must receive God's fresh manna, His holy Word. Daily devotion is what we think of as the quiet time with God. This is a must if we are to be victorious.

Fidelity is needed in our devotional life, because true faithfulness can only be attained as we draw our strength from heavenly manna.

Strength and joy are found in daily meditation as we come to God alone before we meet the duties of the day. Only as we draw from God's limitless grace can we be kept from sinning.

We are responsible to keep our lives in order; no one else can do it for us.

Satan knows how very important our personal devotion is in our life; therefore, he is there to hinder or destroy our quiet time with God. Circumstances, situations, or atmosphere are not the real problem. It is self that Satan uses to undermine our effectiveness.

Just as manna in the wilderness lasted only for a day, so in our personal devotion to God, His manna only gives strength and direction for that day. Each day, we, too, must ask God for a fresh supply. "As the hart panteth after the water brooks, so panteth my soul after thee, O God. My soul thirsteth for God, for the living God. . . . When I remember these things, I pour out my soul . . ." (Psalm 42:1, 2a, 4a).

Do I really desire God and search in His Word for strength and refreshment as the deer that has been chased by its enemy and now finally reaches safety and a clear, cool water brook where it drinks long and deeply? So must we also draw strength and courage from God's Word because we, too, are in enemy territory.

Amy Carmichael, in her book *Edges of His Ways,* says it well concerning manna. "First the morning dew fell, then the manna on the dew, then the dew again over the manna."

If this was the way it was for the children of Israel, this is a wonderful resemblance of our daily manna, too. First prayer in quietness, praising and thanking God for who He is. Then we read God's Word (our manna). Next, in thanksgiving, we ask and make our petitions known to Him.

If this is our experience, then the day will be filled with gratitude to our heavenly Father and service to our fellowman. Throughout each day we will be surrounded by God in quietness and reverence.

The story is told of a lady who went to a famous physician for advice about her ill health. She was a person of nervous temperament. During her visit, she gave the doctor a list of her symptoms. He made a very brief reply, 'Go home and read your Bible an hour each day, then come back in a month from today." He dismissed her before she could protest.

Anger was her first reaction, but she realized that at least the prescription was not expensive. She determined to read her neglected Bible faithfully. When she went back to her doctor a month later, she seemed like a different person. How did he know what she needed?

Pointing to a well-worn and marked open Bible, his reply was, "If we omit daily Bible reading, we lose the greatest force of strength and skill given to us by God."

Goals for a Discreet Life . . .
Say no unkind word about anyone. Be gracious to family and friends alike. Glorify God by speech and way of life. Keep the work done promptly. Keep a mental list of tasks to do in the future . . . so God's word is not dishonored.

(Taken from Titus 2:5)

Slow Me Down, Lord

Slow me down, Lord.

Ease the pounding of my heart by quieting my mind.

Steady my hurried pace with a vision of the eternal reach of time.

Give me, amid the confusion of the day, the calmness of the everlasting hills.

Break the tensions of my nerves and muscles with the soothing music of the singing streams that live in my memory. Help me to know the magical, restoring power of sleep.

Teach me the art of taking minute vacations—of slowing down to look at a flower, to chat with a friend, to pat a dog, to read a few lines from a good book.

Slow me down, Lord, and inspire me to send my roots deep into the soil of life's enduring values, that I may grow toward the stars of my greater destiny.

Courtesy of the Baxter Lane Company, Armarillo, TX, 1975.
Used by permission.

3

Chew Your Food Well!

A young couple and their one-year-old baby were among our guests one Sunday evening. As the mother prepared the food for her little girl to eat, she patted the baby's head and said, "Chew your food well!"

It reminded me that my heavenly Father also expects me to chew my food as I meditate and study His Word. Only as I partake of His Word and make it a part of my life will His Word be of any benefit to me.

Just as chewing our food properly is essential for our digestive system, the same is true in our spiritual life. We must read God's Word with a deep love and devotion in our hearts for our Master. Then our minds and our hearts will be open to receive His truth. "With my whole heart have I sought thee: O let me not wander from thy commandments. Thy word have I hid in mine heart that I might not sin against thee" (Psalm 119:10, 11).

Many of us have experienced the excitement of a young child eagerly anticipating a good meal. What enthusiasm is shown as the food cools to taste! Does God see eagerness and excitement in my Christian life? Is there enthusiasm when the Bible is read? Does God's Word become a part of my life? Does God see growth in my life? We become very concerned when our little children lose their appetite, or when they are satisfied with only milk. Their growth is stunted. How much more is our heavenly Father concerned that we love Him and enjoy His Word and make it a part of our life! A sluggish spiritual appetite also indicates that one is stunted and sickly by reading little or nothing or just reading because we feel that we must.

I like the rendering in *The Living Bible*. It describes this kind of person: "You have been Christians a long time now, and you ought to be teaching others, but instead you have dropped back to the place where you need someone to teach you all over again the very first principles of God's Word. You are like babies who drink only milk, not old enough for solid food. And when a person is still living on milk it shows he isn't very far along in the Christian life, and doesn't know much about the difference between right and wrong. He is still a baby-Christian! . . . Let us stop going over the same old ground again and again. . . . Let us go on instead to other things and become mature in our understanding, as strong Christians ought to be . . ." (Hebrews 5:12-14, Hebrews 6:1a).[1]

Just as we are concerned that babies grow and mature, so much and much more does God desire for us to grow up. We can only grow up and mature in our Christian life as we feed on God's all-sufficient nourishment.

Our hearts must be renewed and pricked by God. "Now when they heard [these things] they were pricked in their hearts and said . . . what shall we do? [Peter told them] Repent . . . and ye shall receive the gift of the Holy Ghost" (Acts 2:37, 38). In obedience and love to God, we will be sensitive to meet all of God's requirements.

As we continue to know God's Word and as we chew our spiritual food well, we will also share with the disciples the Emmaus road experience. "Did not our heart burn within us, while [Jesus] talked with us by the way, and while he opened to us the scriptures?" (Luke 24:32). Only then can this poem be our testimony:

---

1. *The Living Bible* (Wheaton, Illinois: Tyndale House Publishers, 1971).

The Precious Bible

Though the cover is worn
And the pages are torn
Though places bear traces of tears,
Lots more precious than gold
Is the Book worn and old
That can shatter and scatter my fears.

When I prayerfully look
In the precious old Book,
Many pleasures and treasures I see
Many tokens of love
From the Father above
Who is nearest and dearest to me

This old Book is my guide
It's a friend by my side,
It will lighten and brighten my way,
And each promise I find
Soothes and gladdens my mind,
As I read it and heed it each day.

—Author Unknown

No Life Is Lived in Vain

No one lives in vain for Jesus
Let this truth sink in your mind.
As you labor in His vineyard
Doing well your work assigned
Keeping patience through your trials
Seeking not a place to quit;
Till you are called to come up higher
Where the true and faithful sit.

"Therefore, my beloved [sisters], be ye stedfast, unmoveable, always abounding in the work of the Lord, forasmuch as ye know that your labour is not in vain in the Lord" (I Corinthians 15:58).

—Author unknown

4

All, All, All

No ruler or emperor has ever demanded such total dedication as God does. "Thou shalt love thy God with *all* thine heart, and with *all* thy soul, and with *all* thy might" (Deuteronomy 6:5, italics added).

It is important that we understand the cost of total dedication or discipleship. When we think of a disciple, we generally think of a learner or a follower. The definition of the Greek word brings out a more meaningful thought, "one who accepts his instruction and makes it the rule of his life." This means commitment to Christ with no reservations.

We may think of ourselves as Christians, but unless we meet the requirements of God, we will find ourselves weighed in a balance and found wanting (Daniel 5:27). Only the one who truly believes is obedient, and only the one who is obedient truly believes.

Following are several questions that test our honesty to the lordship of Christ:

1. Do I accept Jesus' instructions, and is that the rule of my life?

2. Is Jesus first on my list of priorities and above any earthly relationship I have?

3. Do I value my commitment to Christ more than I do my selfish ambitions?

4. Is the cross of Jesus a joy? Do I count all else as nothing?

5. Have I forsaken all to follow Christ whole-heartedly? "He that loveth father or mother . . . son or daughter . . . more than me is not worthy of me. And he that taketh not his cross, and followeth after me, is not worthy of me. He that findeth his life shall lose it: and he that loseth his life *for my sake* shall find it" (Matthew 10:37-39, italics added).

Discipleship is the heart of the matter and is a matter of the heart. We dare not be careless in our commitment to Christ in our daily living. Every day must be a serious day.

Our life is an open book before God. Therefore, it is impossible to hide anything because God sees right into the deepest recesses of our heart.

Moses met God at the burning bush (Exodus 3:1-2). In Exodus 4:2, God asked Moses what he had in his hand, to which Moses replied, "a rod." That was Moses' only possession, and God asked him to cast it upon the ground. It became a serpent, but when God told Moses to pick it up, Moses obeyed. The rod became "God's rod." We, too, must obey God and surrender our only (best-loved) possession, our *all* to the Lord, by casting it at Jesus' feet. Then our life will become a vessel through which God's love flows to our fellowmen.

There is no person as free as the person who has given *all* to the lordship of Christ. "He that hath the Son hath life; and he that hath not the Son of God hath not life" (I John 5:12). To many, the term *Lord* has lost its significance. Jesus must be both Lord and Saviour, or He is not Lord at all.

Acts 10:13-15 records a vision that Peter had: "And there came a voice to him, Rise, Peter; kill, and eat. But Peter said, Not so, Lord; for I have never eaten any thing that is common or unclean." "Not so, Lord" is a phrase that should not be found in the genuine Christian's vocabulary. We cannot say "No" and have Jesus as Lord of our life. Either we refuse Jesus' lordship or else Jesus is *Lord of all!*

I Corinthians 15:28, "And when all things shall be subdued then shall the Son also himself be subject unto him that put *all* things under him, that God may be *all* in *all*" (italics added). Surrendering *all* to the lordship of Christ is an individual matter. Surrender means breaking the husk of my stubborn independence to God. It is not having my own ideas, but absolute loyalty and obedience to Jesus. Very few of us know about loyalty for Christ's sake. Not until I deliberately sign away my rights do I become a disciple of Jesus, following carefully and making Him the ruler of my life.

When Jesus is Lord of *all*, He gives a new dimension of love—sacrificed, agape love. The love of God is the highest and deepest love that can prevail. Therefore, when this love is present, the love of husband and wife and family members will know a secure love, a love that is not swayed by circumstances. Since agape love is a selfless love, our love is rooted and settled there. God will also bless with *phileo* or physical love. Since many individuals and families allow self and *phileo* love to be their first concern, their love diminishes. When Christ is Lord, the godly love makes the difference. It is this agape love that enables individuals and couples to become more Christlike because God is their foundation.

If Jesus is Lord, then our life is disciplined, structured, and organized day by day, pressing toward the goal of godliness, since becoming like Jesus is a process.

One husband said to his wife, "I could not love you half as much if I would not love Jesus most!" For the Christian wife who has surrendered everything to the lordship of Christ, there is no greater security than such a love.

"All, all, all" is so inclusive! In Matthew 28:18-20, God gives *all* power to live victoriously to those who acknowledge their weakness. His strength knows no limit! He gives unbounded grace to *all* people when *all* things are obeyed. Then only can God's presence, the unceasing fellowship of Christ, be ours *alway*.

All, all, all alway!

Christ in the Home

*Give us homes that God has founded, give us homes with
　　love unbounded;
　Give us homes where Jesus' presence can be felt;
Give us homes where father, mother, son and daughter, sister,
　　brother,
　All in prayer to God the Father oft have knelt.*

*Give us homes where faith is treasured; give us homes where joy
　　is measured
By time and the devotion paid the Word;
Give us homes where love is yearning for the soon returning;
　Give us homes where lives are centered in the Lord.*

—H. H. Savage

5

Family Altar—
The Center of the Home

"O Lord our Lord, how excellent is thy name in all the earth!" (Psalm 8:1). Can it be said of your home that God is the halo, that God is the luminous radiation of glory that surrounds your life as an individual, and that which surrounds your family?

In order to enjoy the blessings of a family altar, a deep devotion and dedication must be the heartthrob of both parents. As always, God has some requirements, too.

1. Our hearts *must* be cleansed from all self-seeking by the blood of Jesus.

2. Our focus *must* be for glorifying God and for the advancement and blessing of our family.

3. All selfish ambition and vanity *must* be brought to Calvary. These tend to bog us down when we bow in prayer in our personal relationship with God.

4. Our soul *must* seek God in everything. This is only found as we meet God on a daily schedule.

Then in such an attitude of personal worship, parents bring into the home the wonderful attribute of the family altar—the daily meeting of God and family.

Ezekiel reminds us in Chapter 44:5, ". . . mark well, and behold with thine eyes, and hear with thine ears *all* that [God says] unto thee concerning *all* the ordinances . . . *all* the laws . . . mark well the entering . . . [and the] going forth . . ." (italics added). Parents are commanded to spell our clearly the boundaries and limits, with eyes and ears that take notice, and to see intellectually; giving individual attention to all the commandments and ways of God. Only then will they become a part of their children. God also holds parents responsible concerning the "goings and the comings." Even our entrances and exits must bring glory to God.

Ezekiel 41:22b mentions "the table that is before the Lord." Exodus 25:30 says, "And thou shalt set upon the table shewbread before me alway." Both references describe the tabernacle, a type of our home. God keeps returning to the center point as His dwelling place with His people. This also reminds us that a man lives his whole life in God's divine presence. Worship is just the same as in Ezekiel's day, a mere form devoid of blessing, if our lives are not found in accordance with God's standard of obedience and holiness

When family worship is in true obedience and holiness, God enables the family to worship Him "in spirit and in truth" (John 4:24). Just as God was concerned that the tabernacle was holy, without sin, so He is concerned that our family worship is a holy place where the whole family can experience the same glory of the Lord that enabled Ezekiel to see God's glory. It is still God's desire to fill our tabernacle, too, with His presence.

It takes effort to have a meaningful, scheduled family worship, but the value far outweighs the determination that it requires. At times we get the idea that once our children are teenagers it will be easier to be on schedule. Or we reason that we will wait until later. But there is never a better time than now.

For babies and small children, family worship can be their "little church" where they learn to sit still and to refrain from loud noises.

Several years ago, we were faced with having one of our girls change jobs. This meant earlier rising or no family devotions and breakfast together. We chose to adapt to her schedule, to get up earlier and have breakfast and family devotions together. We still struggle at times to meet her schedule, but some time ago our daughter told me, "I'll miss breakfast, but I would rather not miss family worship." That was the encouragement we needed again to get our priorities in order.

In the morning before the family goes in various directions, it is such a blessing to gather around a table for breakfast and worship. Someone suggested that the Bible be part of the morning meal. What a blessing to read God's Word and pray for each family member as they face another new day!

There are different ways to make family worship effective. A portion of Scripture can be read by taking turns reading, or else one person can be in charge. Supplements such as the *Daily Bread* or *The Upper Room* can be valuable. *Daily Devotional Treasure* is another daily reading that stimulates thinking.

For small children, daily devotions should be simple, brief, and reverent. As children grow older, they can learn to contribute. This is where the parents' private devotions become a blessing and challenge to their children. Share with the family an outstanding verse that has been a blessing, or ask a question that would stimulate the children's thinking.

Perhaps for some families, different hours of the day would better fit their schedule. Some would think of sitting in the living room for family worship as being more reverent.

Praying is also very important. Bowing heads is one way, but kneeling is more reverent. Why is it that many people kneel with their backs turned toward each other? We were challenged years ago about praying in such a manner. The suggestion was given to form a circle facing each other. The coffee table in our living room served as the family altar when we would all kneel around, forming a circle. Standing in a circle holding hands can also be a blessing for a family. Of course the mode is not so important as that we worship God and please Him.

The phone can be a disturbing factor. Some choose to disconnect it during their worship, while others choose not to.

At times a mother finds herself totally responsible for family devotions when the husband is absent or perhaps on a phone call. It has been our conviction that if Bennie is not present, I will take charge. When our children were small, they would share by reading sentences or phrases in the portion that was read. Sometimes they shared in sentence prayers or led in prayer. As they became older, they would take turns choosing a portion to read and make at least one comment. This was planned in advance and did not come as a surprise.

Charles Finney made the comment years ago, "If parents teach and read the Bible without application, this is worse than no teaching at all." The results will bring inevitable injury to the hearers, because truth separated from life is not truth in the biblical sense.

The reason we are to be consistent in family devotions is because this is one way to introduce our children to the Bible way of life. Paul reminds us "That Christ may dwell in your hearts by faith; that ye, being rooted and grounded in love, May be able to comprehend . . . the breadth, and length, and depth, and height; And to know the love of Christ . . . [being] filled with all the fulness of God" (Ephesians 3:17-19).

A. W. Tozer shared a concern about the difference from the present-day people and that of our forefathers. The forefathers were concerned about the "root of the matter" and present-day people seem only concerned about "the fruit." For that reason, it is an awesome responsibility which we dare not neglect. During family worship, we are silently yet powerfully instilling conviction into the lives of our children. We must be diligent to inspire them in the ideals of God's Word. The Bible is a book of exhortation based upon facts. The greatest portion is devoted to urgent effort to persuade people to alter their ways and to bring their lives into harmony with the will of God.

The proverb "Seeing is believing" is so true in family worship and our relation to God in everyday encounters.

Therefore, we must be those who not only profess Jesus, but we must possess Christ so "that we may present [our children perfectly loyal] in Christ Jesus" (Colossians 1:28).

A Husband's Prayer

Lord, teach me that sixty minutes makes an hour, sixteen ounces a pound, and one hundred cents a dollar. Help me live such a life of integrity that I can lie down at night with a clean conscience. Grant me a wholesome desire to earn an honest living, but deafen me to the jingle of tainted money. Blind me to the faults of my family, but reveal to me my own. Guide me so that each night when I look across the dinner table at my wife I shall have nothing to conceal. Keep me young enough to laugh with little children and sympathetic enough to be considerate of old age. So when I come to the bend in the road and I relive my life, may I be able to take a backward look of life with few regrets. Because I know that "a good name is rather to be chosen than great riches" (Proverbs 22:1).

6

Husband—the Umbrella

Did you ever see a man receive a flagrant insult, only turn a little pale, then give a meek answer? This is the description of a spiritually strong man. Or did you see a man in anguish stand, as if he was carved of solid rock, mastering himself? What about a man bearing the toils of the day yet never boasting of his endurance. That is strength! He who with strong passions remains chaste, keenly sensitive, with manly powers of indignation in himself, can be provoked and yet restrain himself and forgive—that is a truly strong man, a spiritual hero.

Consistency, integrity, caution, and a desire to be right carried out in practice, are to human character what truth, godly fear, and love are to religion. Such virtues can never be reproached. These are the characteristics of a godly husband who is an umbrella for his wife and children.

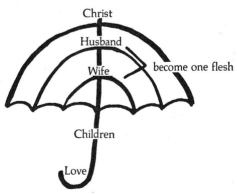

God does not require one thing of His children without also giving specific instructions. The Bible has answers for any question we may face.

In Genesis 18:19 God gives a striking testimony of a husband who was a godly leader, therefore an umbrella: "I know him [Abraham], that he will command his children and his household after him, and they shall keep the ways of the Lord. . . ." Abraham followed God carefully and faithfully. He carried out God's plan precisely.

Noah is another example. "Noah found grace in the eyes of the Lord . . . Noah was a just man and perfect in his generations, and Noah walked with God" (Genesis 6:8, 9). "Thus did Noah; according to *all* that God commanded him, so did he" (Genesis 6:22, italics added). Through Noah's obedience to God, his family was safe and secure during the flood that destroyed every living person except eight souls (Genesis 7:23b).

Job is another example of "a perfect and an upright man, one that feareth God and escheweth evil" (Job 1:8). He was a priestly husband, representing his family to God. "Job sent and sanctified them, and rose up early in the morning, and offered burnt offerings . . . for Job said, It may be that my sons have sinned. . . . Thus did Job continually" (Job 1:5). Even though Job was "the greatest of all the men in the east," he had his priorities straight: God first, his family's spiritual well-being second, then his business. Everything was in its proper place. No wonder Satan was jealous and plagued Job! Job is a noteworthy example for husbands today who are serious about their role.

In John 4:43-54 we read the account of a nobleman who came to Jesus. He pleaded for help because his son was dying. Jesus told the nobleman, "Go thy way, thy son liveth" (verse 50). The man returned to his home having faith in Jesus' words. As a result, the son was healed, the nobleman believed, and so did "his whole house" (verse 53).

Acts 10:2 challenges us with a godly example of a praying husband and father. Cornelius was a centurion, "a devout man, and one that feared God with all his house, which gave much alms to the people, and prayed to God alway."

Acts 16:25-34 relates the beautiful story of the conversion of the jailer who was brought to repentance because Paul and Silas prayed and sang praises to God even though they had been cast into the inner prison and their feet made fast in the stocks. The jailer was in the process of committing suicide when Paul cried with a loud voice, "Do thyself no harm: for we are all here" (verse 28). The Philippian jailer took the men, washed their stripes, and set meat before them. He rejoiced, believing in God with *all* his house.

It is an unmatched blessing for the family if the husband is a godly head and leads *all* the members of his family into the Christian faith.

When faith in God becomes the way of life for the head, it is usually shared by all the family. Because he believes, they all believe. Pardon, peace, and rejoicing are all products of one man taking God's Word seriously.

In order for the husband to be an umbrella for his family, he must be Spirit-controlled. "Walk in the Spirit and ye shall not fulfill the lust of the flesh" (Galatians 5:16). "For as many as are led by the Spirit of God, they are the sons of God" (Romans 8:14). If God is permitted to lead the husband, he will not be swayed by mood swings. We dare not be congenial and cheerful when circumstances are right, then be critical and curt when situations are the opposite. Moody people do have an effect on others, and husbands have a great influence on those closest to them.

Acts 27:25 regards Paul as a good example of one who did not allow his moods to fluctuate with circumstances. It had been the fourteenth day of fasting for Paul and the ship crew because of a tempestuous sea. Paul encouraged them, "Be of good cheer: for I believe God...." There is no greater comfort and security than when the husband believes God and acts upon that.

Husbands have a great influence in creating stable moods in the home. Irritation and bad moods must be confessed as sin and forsaken. Spiritual fidelity is imperative.

Often the children mirror the moods of their dad; therefore, one must die to self and live unto God so that children can *respond* positively rather than *react* negatively.

As "iron sharpeneth iron" (Proverbs 27:17), so God's Spirit must be allowed to polish and beautify the inner life by responding properly in the home.

Just as the umbrella has two positions, so the husband has the choice to be a protection for his family or else be concerned only about himself.

Jonah, for example, was controlled by his selfish moods. Instead of obeying God and rejoicing, he pouted and complained (Jonah 4:1-4).

When the husband is an umbrella, his family will have a restful and secure place to live. They will not fear because "in the fear of the Lord is strong confidence" (Proverbs 14:26). The home will be free from friction and confusion because the husband is constantly receiving his direction from his Head, the Lord Jesus. Since friction results from selfishness, no "little sins" are found because the umbrella continually shelters the family from the ever-present worldly surroundings. Contentment and fulfillment reign because their treasures are laid up in heaven (Matthew 6:33). Plenty of spiritual food is always available; therefore, there is no hunger or hankering after the things of this world. There is no jealousy or envy because all are equal and loved for who they are. Joy and peace are the elements that reign since faithfulness in all things is so important (Luke 16:10a).

Genesis 20:16 describes the husband as an umbrella: "... behold, he is to thee a covering of the eyes." Therefore, the ever-living Christ is here to bless. The nearer you live to God, the nearer you will be to each other in your family.

Excerpt from a message preached at Pilgrim Church by Ray Stutzman, Plain City, Ohio, October 28, 1990. Used by permission.

Prayer in the Kitchen

Lord of all pots and pans and things,
    Since I've no time to be
A saint by doing lovely things, or
    Watching late with Thee,
Or dreaming in the dawnlight, or
    Storming heaven's gates,
Make me a saint by getting meals and
    Washing up the plates.

Although I must have a Martha's hands,
    I have a Mary's mind;
And when I black the boots and shoes,
    Thy sandals, Lord, I find.
I think of how they trod the earth
    What time I scrub the floor;
Accept this meditation, Lord,
    I haven't time for more.

Warm all the kitchen with Thy love, and
    Light it with Thy peace.
Forgive me all my worrying, and make
    All grumbling cease.
Thou who didst love to give men food,
    In room or by the sea,
Accept this service that I do—
    I do it unto Thee.

Courtesy of Back to the Bible broadcast, Lincoln, NE.
Used by permission.

7

A True Counterpart

How much of the world's success and prosperity is contained in the compass of the words of this poem! The power of a wife for good or evil is immense! She makes home the domain of joy and contentment, or joy is altogether unknown. A wife who is a true counterpart to her husband is an encouragement to her family, strengthening them to perform what is right. She gives hope and is an example in endurance. Godly wisdom is in her mouth. She ministers at the very fountain of life and happiness. It is her hand that pours out with an overflowing cup its soul-refreshing waters. Her ardent spirit breathes the breath of life into all enterprises. Her patience and constancy are instrumental in carrying forward to completion the work of God. Her moral sensibility is an unseen power which is at work to build the family that will bring glory to God and contribute to the church and society. Her hands are trained to intelligence, virtue, and love. She makes her home a place of contentment and a place where her family loves to be.

In creation, God planned that man would subdue the earth, and the woman would be his helper. Together, they would be complete. *Counterpart*, according to Webster, is a "thing that fits another perfectly; one who completes or complements."

The first step in becoming a true counterpart is to accept the gift of regeneration which is bestowed sovereignly by God. Regeneration is one of the attributes of God. Only as God's righteousness is bestowed by Christ upon our lives can we be brought into sinless perfection. This is the only way a sinless person can stand before a sinless God. God sees the believer through the righteous blood of Christ.

A true counterpart is more than just a helper. She has chosen the vocation of wife and mother; therefore, she is diligent to learn and grow in all areas of this role. An example could be to work as if one were aiming for the Presidency.

Proverbs 31:10-31 describes the wonders of a good counterpart. She is a virtuous woman having strength of character. The fear of God is her first concern. Her spirit is one of reverence, and the life she lives is one of worship and adoration to her heavenly Father. She studies daily and diligently to find God's perfect will. She finds contentment at home, since she knows her heart and home are God's sanctuary. Constantly and earnestly are the ways she lives, because she is well aware that the joy and security of her home depend upon the favor and blessing of her heavenly Father. Purity marks her thoughts and actions. She gives her whole heart and life for the sake of her husband and children. She is faithful to God and her family even in the little, unnoticed, and hidden areas of life. This makes her life pure and holy because she has nothing to hide.

The true counterpart is tireless in pursuing her responsibilities. Even though she becomes tired physically, she never tires of or dreads her God-given responsibility.

The virtuous woman has no time for idle talk. She does not nag, nor is her speech degrading. Because she is familiar with the laws of God, she knows the secret of lasting joy. Therefore, she guides her children in God's way, and instills heaven-bound wisdom into their minds early in life.

Compassion and kindness describe her way of life. By gentleness and encouragement she reaches out to friends and neighbors alike, giving constant comfort and cheer. Since she plans ahead, she is not frustrated when she is faced with interruptions. Instead, she finds joy even in the unpleasant tasks because she views each situation from God's point of view.

Integrity is her watchword, making her honest in all business and personal matters.

Strength and dignity are her characteristics. She has an undivided loyalty.

In meekness she stands by her husband, living the truth of God's Word.

She is a woman of a meek and quiet spirit. Love and esteem are woven in her character. Her influence is felt more often than recognized, even after her face and voice are no longer seen and heard.

The true counterpart can think of the future and still not worry or be fearful, because she knows that God is already there. If she is faithful today, God's grace will be her strength tomorrow.

Because of her diligence at home, her husband is able to minister to other needs and fulfill God's call in church responsibilities or abroad.

She is faithful in holding the faith of Christ. She lives by His principles and is guided by His Spirit, fulfilling His law of love.

Her life is a life of prayer, since she knows that prayer is the key that unlocks the door of God's grace and His manifold blessings.

The true counterpart chooses to be cheerful even though circumstances may not always be ideal. She avoids extremes. "Even-keel" describes her disposition.

Forgiveness is another virtue. At times, she is misunderstood, envied, or slandered. When these wrongs are confessed to her, she keeps on loving, even though at times it may appear hard to love, since "loving is the bond of perfection" (Colossians 3:14-15). The peace of God rules her heart and life; therefore, thanksgiving is her response. God's love flows through her life to others around her, because Jesus' blood has made her a pure and clean channel through which God can bless others.

She is one who gives, and gives, and gives again, with no thought of repayment. Since selfishness has ended at Calvary, she has no rights of her own.

God's plan for the virtuous woman is to spend her lifetime serving others. The young wife serves her husband children and later her aging parents. Older women train and assist the younger to pursue motherhood and encourage them when their tasks seem wearisome and endless. Serving from the heart of love makes duty a delight. Since charity begins at home, it is an opportunity and a ministry rather than a profession.

Homemaking is not a meager chore. It is a lifetime commitment. Humble? Yes! But she who humbles herself will be exalted (Matthew 23:11, 12).

Submission is another virtue that has been defined as "to work under and for her head's best interest, in obedience to God." Since a virtuous wife is of strong character, she will have her life in command. Therefore, she is able to encourage her husband to be all God wants him to be. Even though she is a discreet wife, she will gladly submit to her husband's discretion. (He is her final authority under God.)

Since she is virtuous woman, she marks well her bulwarks (is very concerned) about the home because her influence reaches generations to come (Psalm 48:13, paraphrased). Then she claims the following verse, "For this God is our God for ever and ever: he will be our guide even unto death" (Psalm 48:14).

The world is watching, and we dare not disappoint God by refusing to be a true counterpart. If we fail, we are encouraging the world to reject God's Word (Titus 2:5).

What a privilege to be counted worthy by God to live

under the commanding influence of God's principles, breathing His Spirit, and shedding a Christian influence in our home and in the church community where we live.

What is more blessed than doing the most excellent work of God by filling an honorable and useful sphere—that of being a true counterpart?

My Family Follows Me

A careful man I want to be:
For my family follows me.
I do not dare to go astray
For fear they'll go the selfsame way.

I cannot once escape their eyes;
Whate'er they see me do they try;
Like me they say they're going to be—
For my family follows me.

They think that I am good and fine;
Believe in every word of mine.
The bad in me they must not see—
For my family follows me.

I must remember as I go,
Through summer's sun and winter's snow,
I'm building for the years to be
For my family follows me.

—*Author unknown*
adapted by Shirley Byler

8

Follow the Leader

As I drove along the interstate, black, fierce clouds indicated that a thunderstorm was approaching. Several minutes later, rain came down in sheets, making it nearly impossible to see the vehicle ahead. The red taillights dimly revealed the car's location and movements. Occasionally the turn signal would blink, alerting me to change lanes. Taking a glance in the rearview mirror and checking both sides of the car, I carefully maneuvered the car to continue following the vehicle ahead.

When we finally arrived at our destination, it was with a grateful heart that I turned off the ignition. I expressed my thankfulness to my heavenly Father and to my husband who made it as easy as he could for me to follow him.

This incident reminded me of God's order for husband and wife. Husbands are commanded to follow Christ their head and love as He loved the church. Wives are to submit and follow, and husbands to love and lead.

Some years ago, Brother Ervin Hershberger related an account of a bride and groom at their premarital counseling session that has been a challenge to me. He said that the bride, with meekness and humility, looked into her future husband's eyes and said, "I will follow you as you follow Christ." What a commitment and what a challenge to search our own lives to see how strong our own commitment is. Since the husband is to follow Christ and the wife is to follow her husband, there will be no competing, rivalry, envy, or strife because the two are content when their eyes are fixed on Jesus.

God expects that there are clear goals and patterns in marriage. If I could not have followed the vehicle my husband was driving by watching the turn signals or brake lights, or if he would have given opposite directions from what he planned, or if he would not have had "home" as our goal, I could not have followed at all.

It is of utmost importance that leaders and followers remain balanced in this world of extremes. We must develop inner strength and godly character and peace in a world of weakness and uncertainty.

If followers are to know how to perform, the leader must know and clearly define the goal or explain what he means. A good leader knows why he does what he does; therefore, he will lead clearly and plainly so it is easy to follow. The Bible tells us in Matthew 15:14, "...if the blind lead the blind, both shall fall into the ditch." In Amos 3:3, we are asked the question, "Can two walk together, except they be agreed?"

In order to be worthy of our calling as leaders and followers, we must be sensitive to God's call, to do God's bidding in God's way.

Therefore, it takes a *clear mind:* "Let this mind be in you, which was also in Christ Jesus" (Philippians 2:5).

A *cheerful disposition* is necessary: "Being filled with the fruits of righteousness unto the . . . praise of God" (Philippians 1:11).

A *discreet mouth* is also important. "Set a watch, O Lord, before my mouth; keep the door of my lips" (Psalm 141:3).

We need *keen judgment* to be able to discern God's will. "The fear of the Lord is the beginning of wisdom" (Proverbs 9:10). In order to make proper decisions and choose the best, the must keep our hearts "with all diligence; for out of it are the issues of life" (Proverbs 4:23).

Humility is also of great importance. "Let nothing be

done through strife or vain glory; but in lowliness of mind let each esteem other better than themselves" (Philippians 2:3).

We must continually be aware that our example outlines our profession.

Unknown to many, there are those who are following the example they see. Leaders are training other leaders. As wives and followers, we are also training others by the example of how we follow our leader.

How important that influence is passed on!

With Psalm 23 as a guide, I have paraphrased the following:

A True Leader

1. The husband is the leader; the wife shall have no unnecessary frustrations.

2. Since he is the "house-band," the bands are security and peace. Therefore the family enjoys a pleasant, comfortable, godly atmosphere.

3. He does his utmost to draw his family to God. He leads the way in right relationships, first to God, then to others. He shows the family, by example, the way of confession, repentance, and restitution, for God's sake.

4. There are times when his wife faces severe trials, and is tempted in anguish and calamities, yet her leader points her to God and what is best for her spiritual well-being. Joys and sorrows are mutually shared.

There are times when the rod of discipline and the staff are needed, yet they are always administered in tender love and deep Christian care.

5. Even in the midst of a hostile world, the family enjoys the sweet table of fellowship and devotion to God, and to each other. Even as olive oil has many different uses, so the wife encourages her leader in many ways to fulfill his important position of headship. Therefore she is blessed, and the blessings cannot all be contained, but overflow to all those around her.

6. God blessed so abundantly . . . there are beautiful

and good things to enjoy; pleasant, favorable, and lovely things are all around. Blessings are abounding in spiritual life as well as in the everyday life. These are all here to enjoy all the days of their life. Best of all to know this is only a foretaste of their heavenly and eternal Home!

Be such a woman, and live such a life,
that if every woman were such as you, and
every life like yours, this earth would
be God's paradise.

Now

If you have hard work to do,
    Do it now.
Today the skies are clear and blue,
Tomorrow clouds may come in view,
Yesterday is not for you;
    Do it now.

If you have a song to sing,
    Sing it now.
Let the notes of gladness ring
Clear as song of bird in Spring.
Let every day some music bring;
    Sing it now.

If you have kind words to say,
    Say them now.
Tomorrow may not come your way.
Do a kindness while you may,
Loved ones will not always stay;
    Say them now.

If you have a smile to show,
    Show it now.
Make hearts happy, roses grow,
Let the friends around you know
The love you have before they go;
    Show it now.

                                    —Anonymous

Courtesy of Sword of the Lord Publishers, Murfresboro, TN, 1969.
Used by permission.

9

Home—Order or Disorder?

"Work well planned is work half done" is a slogan I have learned to appreciate. More recently though, a quote, "I plan my work, but I work God's plan," has become alive. I can plan my work with the stipulation that God is in control, and since He views "the whole," my plans are always subject to change.

Order in the home makes it possible to enjoy living even though we think the day is already fuller than can be contained. There is a calm assurance that the blessings come by working God's plan.

Flexibility is a prerequisite for orderly planning, then working God's plan.

Not only does working God's plan bring an orderly, uncluttered mind, it also brings a submissive heart.

I believe organizing is the only way to bring stability into the home. There is freedom in orderliness, and it is a virtue we so desperately need in a world of confusion and disarray.

At times we may feel bound to disorder and cluttered living. As husbands and wives, we are to help and encourage each other to become more organized. Organization brings release from the pressures of life.

According to Webster, *organization* or *order* is "a process of arranging so the whole works as a unit with each element having a proper function." First it is a process, which means it is always ongoing. We never complete organization. I like to think of "the whole" as the family. There are many functions in the home, yet the chief purpose in all areas is to bring glory to God. So, in order for our homes to function properly, all elements must function properly. There needs to be a continual process of fitting life together in order to have a pleasant and God-centered atmosphere.

To be organized, we need a schedule. At times "no" is applied to requests that conflict with the schedule we feel God would have us establish. Scheduling brings relaxation because it defeats frenzy and hurry.

Order and flexibility bring freedom to begin new tasks or stop old ones without confusion and guilt. We are permitted calmly to switch tasks as situations change because time has been taken to arrange, organize, and schedule without feeling guilty or fearful.

Goals are a must in an orderly home. Goals can be described as tasks that need to be completed. They should be achievable. At times they must be broken into subgoals or objectives, therefore making it easier to reach a certain goal.

"Let all things be done decently and in order" (II Corinthians 14:40). Since God is a God of order, this virtue will also characterize His children.

An orderly home is needed in this disorderly society. It is imperative to arrange family priorities.

God's will must have priority in all that occurs. With God as the center, all other interests will be brought into line to bring glory to Him.

Communication is essential in arranging priorities and order. There must be time allotted so every member can express the feelings of his heart in an atmosphere that is relaxed and caring. Parents must plan time for this all-important growing factor in the orderly home.

Parents must first be convinced that order is needed so the home can function properly. Only then can children be taught and trained to love and appreciate an orderly, well-arranged family unit. Children will not learn order on their own; they must be trained to appreciate an orderly environment. "In thee, O Lord, do I put my trust: let me never be put to confusion" (Psalm 71:1).

Consistency is another valuable ingredient in the orderly home. It is so important to consider prayerfully any issue that arises, then make the decision and stay with the conclusion consistently and humbly. In order to view any situation from God's perspective, we must have His wisdom, the knowledge of His Word, and understand what God's will is (Ephesians 5:17).

Cooperation is also needed. This comes as a result of confidence. Parents must seek for every possible occasion to foster and strengthen cooperation in the home.

Punctuality not only includes being on time, but promptness in meeting every requirement during the day. This requires self-denial and the discipline to resist the temptation to waste time, being willing to sacrifice ease of pleasure for the sake of future and present well-being.

The virtue of neatness, including cleanliness, is a personal duty in every orderly home. This includes not only personal cleanliness, but also neatness in everything that is possessed, used, or done.

Accuracy in word, in work, and in conduct is an essential virtue to order. People must be trained to see, to hear, to think, to remember, to speak, to write, and to perform all duties with accuracy.

The virtue of quietness includes the control of one's natural conduct and impulse to talk. It is possible that more spiritual progress can be made in moments of silence, in the awesome presence of God, than in hours of talking. Quietness makes continuous and fruitful thinking possible.

The virtue of industry involves the steady putting-forth of energy. This development calls for many choices. Especially in the home there are constant demands to keep the seemingly insignificant duties up-to-date. Industry is the discipline which prepares one to "endure hardness" (II Timothy 2:3). Industry does not always bring quick rewards, but Ecclesiastes 9:10 reminds us to do with our might what our hands find to do.

Prompt obedience is the only obedience that God accepts. Slow obedience is no obedience at all; therefore, it is imperative to obey promptly.

Truthfulness is very essential. To lack truthfulness is more than defeat—it spells disaster! Truth must ring loud and clear.

Motivation is important to achieve proper goals. High and worthy motives build strong and noble character. There are two kinds of incentives—natural and artificial. The desire to grow and achieve knowledge is the incentive we desire to be evident. Artificial incentives are largely substitutes for the genuine and direct away from godly desires to self-indulgence.

Proverbs 24:3, 4 gives us the blueprint for an orderly home. "Through wisdom is a house builded; and by understanding it is established. And by knowledge shall the [rooms] be filled with all precious and pleasant riches."

Yes, it is possible to have an orderly home in a disorderly world by planning our work, then working God's plan.

Success

Before God's throne to confess
I knelt and bowed my head.
"I failed," I wailed. The Master said,
"Thou didst thy best—that is success."

Parent's Prayer

O *Heavenly Father, make me a better parent. Teach me to understand my children, to listen patiently to what they have to say, and to answer all their questions kindly. Keep me from interrupting them or contradicting them. Make me as courteous to them as I would have them be to me. Forbid that I should ever laugh at their mistakes, or resort to shame or ridicule when they displease me. May I never punish them for my own selfish satisfaction or to show my power. Let me not tempt my child to lie or steal. And guide me hour by hour that I may demonstrate by all I say and do that honesty produces happiness. Reduce, I pray, the meanness in me. And when I am out of sorts, help me, O Lord, to hold my tongue. May I ever be mindful that my children are children and I should not expect of them the judgement of adults. Let me not rob them of the opportunity to wait on themselves and to make decisions. Bless me with the bigness to grant them all their reasonable requests and the courage to deny them privileges I know will do them harm. Make me fair and just and kind. And fit me, O Lord, to be loved and respected and imitated by my children.*

Courtesy of Baxter Lane Company, Armarillo, TX, 1975
Used by permission

10

Children—Strength
or STRESS?

There are many similarities between teaching our children and the art of gardening. Three basics are needed in both: a vision, a method, and the finished product.

Early in spring, gardeners browse through seed catalogs and check for better techniques. So also in the life of a young couple, it is with great anticipation they shop, plan, and prepare for their new baby. Both have a vision of a perfect plan.

What a blessing to prepare the garden spot, sow the seed, ask God's blessing, and watch the seedlings come through the soft earth as the warm sun and gentle showers keep the ground in perfect condition for growth. If gardeners would stop here, it would not be long until the weeds would take over and choke out the seeds. What a blessing a little baby is, pure, innocent, and "angelic"— but not for long! Babies show their human nature as they want what they want now, with no consideration of their parents. Wise parents hold their babies tightly when they stiffen to show their self-will. Parents gently and consistently instill in them what the word "no" means.

Deuteronomy 6:7 tells us, "And thou shalt teach them diligently unto thy children, and shalt talk of them when thou sittest in thine house, and when thou walkest by the way, and when thou liest down, and when thou risest up." We must shape our children's behavior early. It takes place by consistently teaching, when we walk or travel, while eating, reading to them, or when we work. (Little children should play where the mother works, so they can communicate.) "Every child is fully capable of being 100 percent obedient," says Brother John Risser. He continues, "Perhaps we may excuse low grades in academics, but there is *no* excuse for misbehavior."

In Judges 13:1-14, we read the interesting account of the angel's visit with Manoah and his wife. Manoah asked the angel a challenging question each parent should ask God, "How shall we order the child?" The angel told them to do *all* that God commands, (verse 14). In Deuteronomy 6:5, 6 we find God's command, "And thou [parents] shalt love the Lord thy God with *all* thine heart, and with *all* thy soul, and with *all* thy might . . . these words . . . shall be in thine heart" [italics added]. Only then are we able to teach our children. Just as the angel gave Manoah and his wife some practical instruction, so God also has given us some precise instructions that must be followed. God has promised wisdom to carry out His plan.

No one lacks in having a goal or vision for what we desire, be it for our children or for our garden. Few, though, are willing to pay the price to have proper priorities, or to change goals in order to get the desired results of godly children who will be a strength to our homes, the church, and to the community.

There is a tendency to be too involved in the material pursuits of life, rather than to spend proper time to nurture and train our children.

Psalm 112:1-5 describes the godly home, "Blessed [fully satisfied] is the man [home] that feareth the Lord, that delighteth greatly in his commandments." Children from such homes will be "mighty upon the earth" (verse 2). Mighty children are not mediocre, but will strengthen and uphold the statutes of the Lord; therefore, "the generation of the upright shall be blessed" (verse 2). Verses 3-5 mention that a godly person will have a proper concept of wealth and riches, but righteousness shall be his first concern. He will be one who is generous, gracious, and full of compassion because he guides all his affairs with godly discretion. In a home such as this, parents are able to require prompt obedience from their children, a ready response when called, an answer when spoken to, obedience and following through with instruction. Since parents teach more by their attitudes and by their way of life, it is very important that they live what they teach.

A garden left to itself does not remain weed-free. The lives of children must also be tended with diligence. It is much easier to keep the garden looking clean and productive when tiny weeds are taken care of systematically and promptly. The same is true with children. It is much better to teach and "nip the bud" of sin than to allow misbehavior to become uncontrollable.

Gardens, as well as children, need discipline. Amos 3:2 says, "You only have I known of all the families of the earth: therefore I will punish you for all your iniquities." The family is still special to God. God has planned for its best, father, mother, and children. A unique order! God expects discipline in the family unit. It produces respect for the home as God's perfect plan, which in return results in respect for God and others.

Acknowledging God as supreme is vital in training children. "Except the Lord build the house, they labour in vain that build it" (Psalm 127:1a). God is not building our home unless we communicate and really get through to our children by challenging and arousing the children's minds to see the truth and then to make the truth their own. By obeying and loving God and the family, we are authentically living in the fear of the Lord and living by His commandments on a daily basis.

Amram and Jochebed were good examples of instilling conviction in the heart and life of young Moses. Years later, his decisions affected the children of Israel. Because of his parents' teaching, he chose to suffer affliction with God's children, rather than to enjoy the pleasures of sin for a season because he looked on the reward (Hebrews 11:25). Moses not only had a vision, he also had a method to fulfill God's plan because his goal was to follow God's will. No wonder God gave testimony of Moses "whom the Lord knew face to face" (Deuteronomy 34:10b).

Psalm 144:12 gives a reason for parents to be good examples to their children: "That our *sons* may be as plants *grown up in their youth;* that our *daughters* may be as corner stones, *polished after the similitude of a palace"* (italics added). Certainly we could say, "Blessed [happy] is the [family] whose God is the Lord" (Psalm 33:12).

The stronger the foundation of the home, the greater will be the strength of the children, and more generations following will be blessed. Sons grown up and daughters as polished cornerstones are the finished products! These qualities are the stability and the strength that is needed in generations to come.

Yes, there are many similarities between nurturing children and gardening. Much effort is needed, as well as lots of patience and hard work. But if neglected, both will bring STRESS.

Following is a list of guidelines I've composed for parents of teenagers:

Do's and Don'ts for Parents of Teenagers Who Desire Their Children to Be a Strength!

1. Don't fly off the handle. Stay calm; children need to know how much better things turn out when parents are self-controlled.

2. Don't depend on vacations and luxuries as a crutch when things get rough. Children are real imitators.

3. Do be strict; show who's in authority. Youth need to know that parents give strong support. When parents "cave in," teenagers get scared.

4. Do act your age. Don't dress or try to talk like a teen-ager. It is embarrassing and it looks ridiculous.

5. Do be an example by your life and conduct that God is in control. Teenagers need to believe in One greater and stronger than their problems.

6. Don't allow them to lie, steal, or be cruel. Be hard on them. Explain *why* what they do is wrong! Impress upon them the importance of not repeating such behavior.

7. Don't allow them to go unpunished; administer it. But let them know you still love them even though they let you down. It will make them think twice before they do the same thing again.

8. Don't compromise! Make it clear what you mean and mean what you say. Stand up to them and they will respect you; they really don't want everything they ask for.

9. Be honest. Tell them the truth, no matter what, and be straight about everything. They can take it. It is lukewarm and shady answers that make them uneasy and insecure.

10. Do praise them, please, when they deserve it, and they will be able to handle criticism much easier.

He Leadeth Me

In pastures green? Not always!
Sometimes He who knoweth best, in kindness leadeth me
In many ways where heavy shadows be out of the sunshine,
warm and soft and bright
Out of the sunshine, into the darkest of night
I oft would faint with sorrow and of fright
Only for this—I know He holds my hand
So whether in the green or desert land
I trust although I may not understand.

—Author unknown

11

Reflex of Obedience

The story is told of a young son of a missionary couple in Brazil who was playing under a tree in their yard. Suddenly, the voice of the boy's father rang out clearly and commandingly, "Philip, obey me instantly! Drop to your stomach!" Immediately the youngster did as he was told. "Now crawl toward me as fast as you can!" The boy obeyed. "Stand up and run to the house." Philip responded unquestioningly and ran to his father. As the youngster turned to look back at the tree, he saw a large poisonous snake hanging from a branch, right above where he had been playing.

Because of his "reflex of obedience" his life had been spared. Philip could have hesitated and asked, "Why?" or he could have casually replied, "Wait a minute." But it was his prompt obedience that proved a blessing.

Reflex, according to Webster, is "the power of acting or responding with unique speed; an habitual and predictable way of thinking or behaving."

Luke, Chapter 5, verses 4 through 9, gives an interesting account of obedience. The disciples had fished all night and caught nothing. The next morning Jesus told them, "Launch out into the deep, and let down your nets for a draught." Peter, seemingly, was the spokesman, and he informed Jesus about the previous night. "Master, we have toiled all the night and have taken nothing." Yet he said, "Nevertheless at thy word I will let down the net."

What a wonderful example of the "reflex of obedience"! Like Peter, we may feel we know best, because we have experienced a certain defeat. *Nevertheless*, because God's Word is truth (John 17:17), it is forever settled in heaven. Therefore, it behooves us to obey the truth promptly. In I Samuel 15, we have an account that is striking in its lack of the "reflex of obedience." Saul made excuses for his disobedience, then later he also blamed the people. As a result, he discovered that God means what He says and excuses do not stand. Through disobedience he lost God's blessings, his kingdom, and later he took his own life. Prophet Samuel reminded Saul that "to obey is better than sacrifice" (verse 22). Never will sacrifice suffice when God's Word is to be obeyed.

Peter experienced God's blessings by habitual and predictable behavior. In contrast, Saul failed by taking his own way, not waiting for Prophet Samuel, taking things in his own hands, making excuses, and finally blaming the people for becoming impatient.

When God speaks to us about a matter, our obedience must be prompt and unquestioning. When we respond with prompt, unquestioning obedience, we show the genuineness of our faith in God's Word and the reality of our love for the Lord.

"True faith obeys while doubt delays," is a slogan that we must keep in mind. Since Christ dwells in our hearts by faith, we will be "rooted and grounded in love." Only then are we able to comprehend the breadth, length, depth, and height and to *know* the love of Christ, which passes knowledge, filling us with all the fullness of God (Ephesians 3:17-19).

God told Joshua, "Be strong and very courageous, that thou mayest observe to do according to *all* the law ... turn not from it to the right hand or to the left, that thou mayest prosper [do wisely] whithersoever thou goest" (Joshua 1:7, italics added).

As parents, what is our reflex of obedience? We may

well expect immediate obedience from our children, but does our heavenly Father receive such obedience from us? Since obedience is the foundation in God's Word, it is vitally important. "If the foundations be destroyed, what can the righteous do?" (Psalm 11:3). When we view obedience as the foundation of God's will, we count it a privilege to obey willingly. In God's timetable, someday every person will worship and obey Him (Philippians 2:10). This challenge should constantly dictate our actions to love and obey God to the fullest. Those obeying God are on the winning side now and eternally. Obedience should not be viewed as a "have to," but be done willingly and joyously by God's grace. Someday it will be enforced! But what a joy to serve, love, and obey God faithfully each day of our life.

When I learn to give up my will for God's will, God will bless with the same measure of His power to live obediently and joyously. Therefore, when we surrender in full obedience, we will be blessed by faith in God in the same portion.

Malachi 3:6 says, "For I am the Lord, I change not." What a security to know our heavenly Father does not change! He speaks once; that is sufficient. He always leads and convicts through His Word, but He never blindly condemns.

God gave us His Holy Spirit, His holy Word, and His holy Son. He made every provision for our spiritual welfare. But the choice is up to us whether we heed or not.

When we really love God, we will want to know Him and His will. Then our response will be obedience—cheerful, willing, loving obedience that is the kind of reflex God is seeking.

Teach Me

Teach me, O Lord, to be sweet and gentle
  In all events of life; in
Disappointments, in the thoughtlessness
  Of others, in the insincerity of those
I trusted, in the unfaithfulness of those
  On whom I relied. Teach me to profit by
The suffering that comes across my path.
  May no one be less good for having
Come within my influence; no one less
  Pure, less true, less kind, less noble for
Having been a fellow-traveler in our
  Journey toward eternal life.

Courtesy of Baxter Lane Company, Armarillo, TX, 1975.
Used by permission.

12

Yoked or Tied?

As a child growing up in the horse-and-buggy days, I remember my parents taking a special interest in good quality horses. Several times they bought one that no longer qualified for the racetrack, yet was still a good, high-spirited horse. Since these horses were registered and had good pedigrees, we raised colts for a number of years. What excitement these little, wobbly, "all-legs" creatures brought! But their freedom was short-lived. Mom believed that early, strict discipline would make a good, dependable horse, just as she believed in strict discipline for her offspring.

At only a few weeks old, a halter was put on the colt. Poor thing! It would shake its head, buck, and kick. Mom stayed nearby to make sure no injuries occurred. Over and over again, the halter was put on the colt. Next, the colt was tied with a rope. The colt again kicked, bucked, and tore around until it was completely worn out. All the while, Mom was standing nearby, talking and trying to calm the unruly animal. Again and again the procedure would be repeated, and again and again the colt would resist when pressure was put on its freedom. Because Mom was a strong woman, she did not give up, but looked beyond the discomforts of the present and envisioned a good, dependable horse for years to come.

How much like an unbroken colt is the person who allows circumstances of life to govern his moods! One day

63

he is on cloud nine, and on rock bottom the next day. One day he is joking and laughing, and the next he is depressed and striking out at some innocent person.

Our spiritual maturity is often measured by the way we respond to our circumstances when things go wrong. Do we become depressed and blame others, or do we see God in every situation and allow His grace and strength to carry us through the trying time? Our attitudes toward difficulties reveal whether we have Christ within or merely profess to have Him.

When self-will, self-effort, and self-life end at Calvary, then we will be able to see God in everything. Because our hearts have been made pure by His blood, we no longer cater to self, but instead, ". . . I die daily" (I Corinthians 15:31).

While traveling in Latin America sometime ago, we noted with interest their oxen and cart mode of transportation. It was a beautiful scene to see the two oxen yoked together, walking in unison, sharing the same load, having the same goal. Then another scene comes to mind of another team. One was a mature ox, plodding in sure, steady steps, but beside him was a younger one, resisting, balking, pushing, and shoving. Blisters rubbed on his neck and horns. It was obvious this one was tied, not yoked.

Many times we waste God's precious time by resisting and resenting rather than willingly accepting Jesus' yoke and learning from Him. "Come unto me, all ye that labour and are heavy laden, and I will give you rest. Take my yoke upon you, and learn of me. . . . For my yoke is easy, and my burden is light" (Matthew 11:28-30).

Just as resistance and resentment to authority is punished in our homes, so it is also in God's perspective. God often needs to press the point hard until we learn to give Him our first priority.

Often we could have a much more joyful and blessed life if only we would learn from Jesus and walk lovingly and obediently, because we love our heavenly Father and

we love to do His will.
O Lord, give me a joyful heart,
One that is tried and true
So that when troubles and trials are my lot
I'll still be loving and praising You!

JESUS AND I

I cannot make it alone
The waves dash fast and high;
The fog comes chilling around
And the light goes out in the sky,
But I know that, we too, shall win in the end
Jesus and I.

Coward and wayward and weak
I change with the changing sky,
Today so strong and brave
Tomorrow too weak to fly.
But—He never gives in, so we two, shall win
Jesus and I.

—Author unknown

Life's Challenge

The way is long and often steep
No easy path we find,
To make our lives both strong and deep
A blessing to mankind.
Through difficulties to the stars
Be this our purpose high
And loyal, valiant soldiers be
Whether we live or die.

All those who lean on idle oars
Content to drift along
Will never know life's highest joys
Nor sing the victor's song.
Through difficulties to the stars
May this our watchword be
For those who shun the battle scars
There is no victory.

Great oaks from little acorns grow
But not in one short year.
Through summer's heat and winter's cold
They neither shrink nor fear.
And so may we in life's hard test
Press onward to the goal.
Devote our talents to the best
In body, mind, and soul.

—*Author unknown*

13

Noticed or Noble?

On several occasions, young mothers have mentioned their adjustment when they changed their career. Their earlier jobs included teaching school, secretarial work, or other vocations that called for them to be noticed. One mentioned it was like stepping from the bright sunlight to the dim shadows. Even though the calling of a homemaker is quiet and hidden, it is, nevertheless, a noble calling.

It is important as mothers and homemakers that we learn to "possess outstanding qualities, amid a society that would rather be noticed than be willing to do the unnoticed things of life." God chooses ordinary women to do noble work. Faithfulness to God, even though it is done in ordinary, unnoticed tasks, honors God. In John 15:16 we find the phrase "I have chosen you." This should challenge us to gladly let God have His way. We must be willing to do the noble work of homemaking, rather than preferring a work that is more noticed.

Our life must be characterized by the fruit of the Spirit. Love, joy, and peace need to be our way of life. Longsuffering, gentleness, and goodness pertain to the way we work with our families and people in general. Faithfulness, meekness, and temperance refer to our inward character. We are then equipped to better fulfill that noble work that God calls us to because we have availed ourselves to the grace of God for the task that needs to be accomplished. "But to every one of us is given grace according to the measure of the gift of Christ" (Ephesians 4:7). We must always remember, "I cannot, but God can!"

The woman of Shunem, in II Kings 4:8-17, is a prime example of a noble woman. She was not necessarily noticed by her peers, but she filled her place well in her home. Because she was a noble woman of outstanding qualities, she was not content only to care for her husband, but rather her compassion reached out to others. She had the courage to meet the needs of the man of God who passed that way often and needed a place to rest.

Elisha was so impressed by her actions that he wanted to show her kindness. He asked her what she would desire: "What is to be done for thee? wouldest thou be spoken for to the king, or to the captain of the host?" Her answer is another reason why she is considered a noble woman: "And she answered, I dwell among mine own people" (verse 13). Such a quality is rare indeed! That is the virtue of *contentment*. She had no need, because she found herself as she freely gave to meet the needs of her friends and those in need.

The story is told of a noble man by the name of Gutenberg. He invented the printing press in 1460. It wasn't until years later that Gutenberg stated the reason for his success. In a large dictionary he explained that his work had been done under "the protection of the All-Highest who often reveals to the humble what He conceals from the wise."

Very little is known about Gutenberg. Not a single portrait was made of him during his lifetime. No one even discovered as much as one line of his handwriting. We do know, however, that Gutenberg's printing press made it possible for new ideas to be published and spread. Most of all, his efforts were most keenly felt in Christianity, all because he was willing to do a noble work without recognition.

Nobility does not have to be in the forefront, doing only the great and awesome jobs. Nobility is evident in the character of a meek and quiet spirit that willingly toils even though the deeds go unnoticed.

In Mark 12:41-44, we read the account of the poor widow who humbly placed two mites (which would be less than a penny) into the treasury. Like always, Jesus was observing! Jesus also noticed that some gave much and allowed their giving to be seen, while this poor widow gave "all that she had, even all her living" (verse 44).

The scribes are an example of people who loved to be noticed for their much giving, their much praying, and their pious living. Yet, Jesus was not impressed. He pointed out that they already had all the reward they were going to get (Matthew 6:5).

Recently, we were confronted with a decision. A phone call informed us of the drowning of a young relative, hundreds of miles away. Attempts were made to attend the funeral. Because of the distance, aircraft the only possible way of travel, but the rates were very high. After talking about the incident, we decided there are other ways that comfort and encouragement could be given, even though we could not be there for the funeral. A phone call could be made to share our sympathy with the sorrowing family. We could also let them know our concern by taking time to write and send a sympathy card. This could be read and reread. But somehow what I really wanted to do was to attend the funeral, rather than to be content to do the seemingly little, unnoticed deed. To us, it may seem small and insignificant, but to God, it is His character that shines forth if we are willing to be used and give all the glory.

The noble woman or man remembers yesterday with joy, lives today with enthusiasm, and looks forward to tomorrow with confidence knowing it is God who is being served and, therefore, it is God who will notice and reward noble deeds.

Marriage Takes Three

I once thought marriage took
Just two to make a go,
But now I am convinced
It takes the Lord also.

And not one marriage fails
Where Christ is asked to enter,
As lovers come together
With Jesus at the center.

But marriage seldom thrives
And homes are incomplete
Until He's welcome there
To help avoid defeat.

In homes where Christ is first,
It's obvious to see,
Those unions really work,
For marriage still takes three.

Perry Tanksley, © 1990.
Used by permission.

14

God's Hedge of Protection

It is evident that marriage relationships are deteriorating; therefore, the homes are breaking down in our society. Satan is very busy trying to destroy, but with God's help marriages can be preserved. God can provide the inner force to hold a marriage together. Just as God physically holds the atoms in our body together, He is available to be the unseen strength in the marital union. God is willing to establish and perfect a marriage where He is acknowledged as Lord because He loves His people and He has a purpose in mind. God has promised "a threefold cord is not quickly broken" (Ecclesiastes 4:12b).

It is interesting to note the guidelines that God gave to Adam and Eve in Genesis 2:24, 25, "Therefore shall a man leave his father and mother, and shall cleave unto his wife: and they shall be one flesh. And they were both naked . . . and were not ashamed." Adam did not have parents to instruct him with marriage guidelines. And he and Eve were not tempted to infidelity because they were the only human beings created. But God gave them the blueprint in the first portion of His Word, right at the creation, before there was any transgression or questions. So also today, we must have guidelines and rules early in marriage that are based on God's Holy Word in order for us to be faithful to God and to each other. Are we fully aware of God's wonderful love for us? Even in the twentieth century, God's Word is still the whole truth. It has not and will not change. God is still the third person in marriage.

In Genesis 2:24, 25, the word *leave* commands the husband to leave his parents and all others, and he is to *cleave* to his wife. They are commanded to cleave like two pieces of wood glued together, so close that not even the wedge of unkindness or disloyalty can get between them. Romans 8:31 tells us that "if God be for us, who can be against us?" Paraphrased for husband and wife, "If husband and wife are for each other, even Satan cannot be against them, because God is that inner force that holds them together."

Only then can they experience the unity that God would desire, that of "becoming one flesh." They will be *one* in their individual love for God, *one* in church matters, in understanding God's Word and His will, and together will follow His way. They are *one* in life's vocation, *one* in material and financial pursuits, *one* in building their home and in training their children. Yes, they will be united because God is their eternal God; they are *one* in seeking, trusting, and acknowledging God in everything. God does not demand that the couple think alike, but that they think together.

Mary Pride, in her book *The Way Home*, describes the difference between a Biblical and an intimate marriage. In the biblical marriage, romance is the flower of marriage, not the root. The intimate marriage consists of thrills and excitement; therefore, it is self-centered rather than God-centered. God is the root, that inner force that blesses the unity of a couple with a physical and romantic love that pleases Him. "And they were both naked . . . and were not ashamed" (Genesis 2:25). This is only possible as God is included and His blueprint carefully followed.

Yes! God has a hedge about the faithful family. Job's family is a good example of one who experienced God's blessing. That is why Satan accused God, "Hast not thou made an hedge about him . . . and about all that he hath on every side?" (Job 1:10).

Marriages are made and recognized in heaven, but husbands and wives must maintain their marriage. God gave the foundation and the families, but it is up to us to abide within that hedge of protection. Marriage is meant to be a blessed relationship, but it is up to each couple whether it is a blessing or a strain.

Since God's Word is truth, any slight deviation is to move from the truth. For any individual, husband, wife, or parent, there is a narrow road called truth for all to follow closely. To choose that path and remain on it is to follow God's direction. When we decide to no longer meet *all* God's requirements, we are choosing to leave the path of truth, the hedge of God's protection.

Ephesians 5 gives us some very timely advice. The first step is to follow God as dear children, walking in obedience. We are to love God with all our heart and to live the sacrificial life of Christ. We must confess and forsake *all* sin. We are to live a life of thanksgiving and praise to God by living the fruit of the Spirit: goodness, righteousness, and truth. This is the only way to walk circumspectly, as wise people, being careful to use time carefully and wisely. When God fills the couple, there is no room for selfish pursuits or worldly excitement, but rather they are quiet and live a contented, godly life in God's will. By following God's pattern, it is easy and blessed to submit to one another as husband and wife, in submission to Christ, the Head. Therefore the husband loves his wife and children with the sacrificial love with which Christ loves the church, always desiring and striving for their spiritual well-being.

Job is an outstanding example of one who had a sacrificial love for his family. He offered sacrifices and prayers just in case his family sinned (Job 1:5). No wonder Satan was jealous and envious of all the glory God was receiving! Satan still cannot stand to see a God-fearing family; therefore, he is trying to destroy it yet today. But we need not despair because that same hedge (Job 1:10) is still available for every couple. Every fiery dart of Satan must first pass God's approval before it dare touch us. We can, by God's grace, be protected as we follow God's formula carefully.

In school I learned a rule that is still wise to follow:
Good, better, best
Never let it rest
Until the good is better,
And the better is best!

In marriage, this should be the rule, always to desire to mature and grow in God's likeness, not being satisfied but continually growing in holiness. We dare not desire to live "the springtime of our marriage in the shadows of autumn." Rather, we must enjoy each stage of life, recognizing God's blessings, always pressing toward higher plains of spiritual perfection. As "iron sharpeneth iron" (Proverbs 27:17), so must we polish and encourage each other to become more godly.

We dare not compare our marriage with other marriages. Second Corinthians 10:12 reminds us not to compare ourselves among ourselves, for such people are not wise, although we should learn and grow from the experiences of others. Coveting and sinful fantasizing do not belong to the Christian marriage. Someone suggested that most marriage problems are spiritual problems and are compounded when a couple marries. God is left out; therefore, they pursue their own selfish desires. The answer is not merely to pray more and read the Bible more, or just to go from here and do better. Rather, the answer is to be crucified with Christ (Galatians 2:20). Dying to self and living unto God is the only option that brings joy and peace, allowing Christ total control of our lives.

Our baptismal and marriage vows both included a commitment to God, saying "no" to the world and our selfish desires and "yes" to living for God as long as we live. God holds us accountable for such a commitment. He demands total dedication! Commitment brings communication and communication brings confidence. It is sad that confidence is seemingly a word of the past. Husband and wife can be likened to a lock and key. Together they accomplish their purpose, and apart they are of little value. In their proper role, they are equally important because they complement and complete each other. When couples seek God (Matthew 6:33), it becomes a security because the whole family knows that the central point is always God. There is no confusion because God is loved with *all* the heart and *all* the soul and *all* the mind (Matthew 22:37).

At times we take our spouse or children for granted. We think they should know what we mean, when we really never communicated.

Flattery, flirtation, and suggestive jesting are sins that we dare not give in to. Beware of the power of the tongue! "Death and life are in the power of the tongue" (Proverbs 18:21a). "For out of the abundance of the heart the mouth speaketh" (Matthew 12:34). "Whoso keepeth his mouth and his tongue keepeth his soul from troubles" (Proverbs 21:23). God expects us to be discreet in our speech as well as in our lifestyle. We must be able to hold our peace. "The discretion of a man deferreth his anger" (Proverbs 19:11a). The key for controlling our tongue is found in Ephesians 4:15: "But speaking the truth in love, [we] may grow up in him in all things. . . ." God's love in one's heart is defined as the act of one person seeking the highest good in one's spouse, an unselfish concern for the other's spiritual well-being. With an attitude such as this, we will be humble and quick to confess when we have wronged our spouse or family. We must acknowledge our humanity; therefore, we feel with them and share our desire for them to grow in Christ. Confession is good for the soul!

Consecration to God must be wholehearted. It is in the transformed, consecrated heart where God dwells and Satan is defeated.

When we live and walk in the Spirit (Galatians 5:25), it is evident that God's hedge of protection is about us. We cannot claim to be walking in God's Spirit when we become angry or place blame on our spouse. In doing so, we grieve the blessed Holy Spirit. When problems arise—and they will—each obstacle must be confronted with a cool head and a warm heart. God sees the heart and knows who we are rather than who we pretend to be.

God does not expect us to employ all the gifts of the Spirit, but He does command the Christian to possess all the fruit of the Spirit. When the fruit is absent, we lose our effectiveness in prayer and our witness. God expects us to live a holy life because people are looking for examples to follow. Society is observing families, and faithful ones are a powerful witness for God. Since actions speak louder than words, we are judged largely by our actions. Only then, if needed, we use words as witness.

"Being confident of this very thing, that [God] which hath begun a good work in you will perform it until the day of Jesus Christ" (Philippians 1:6). What a blessing to know it is God who is that inner Strength, that inner Force that holds our marriage together. He has a hedge of protection about the family. Where the blood of Christ is applied, there Christ dwells, and Satan is put to flight. Yes, God is the one who blesses and leads right to the journey's end, and it is He who surrounds us with His hedge of protection along the way.

God has two dwellings—one in heaven
the other in a meek and thankful heart.

Caring for Each Other

Take care of each other, dear Husband and Wife,
  For time is fleeting, there's no time for strife.
Always be faithful and pray for each other,
  For strong is the power of a praying couple.

Take care of each other, dear Husband and Wife,
  When struggles and trials have entered your life.
For then is the time a faithful companion
  To be to each other must never be ended.

Take care of each other, dear Husband and Wife,
  Consider the ungodly, their house is of strife.
Satan has destroyed it, and maliciously craves,
  Your home, your life, and children enslave.

Take care of each other, dear Husband and Wife,
  For Christ in His love for the church gave His life.
He cares for her daily, thru struggles, thru fears,
  For He has once crossed this vale of tears.

Take care of each other, dear Husband and Wife,
  For the night is far spent, eternity is nigh.
Soon comes the cry, the bridegroom is come,
  Then it's too late to do the undone.

—Author unknown

15

Termites in Marriage

What a sense of accomplishment I felt as I straightened my tired back to get a better view of my beautiful, newly waxed hardwood floor. But one thing bothered me. There was a bubble in the floor that I had not noticed before. I mentioned to my husband what I had found. He assured me it was caused by the expansion and contraction of the wood and there was no need to worry. Naturally, I was relieved.

Some months later, I was busy spring cleaning the living room. As I lifted the oval rug, I discovered not only one bubble but a number of bubbled spots. Again I showed my husband the floor. This time, he too was concerned. He arranged to have the termite exterminators to come and take a look at the floor.

The exterminators determined that termites were indeed present, and they set out to remedy the problem. Six-inch ditches were dug all around the foundation of our house, and holes were drilled on the inside walls of the rooms. The entire house was fumigated. In addition to the high cost, there was lots of hard work, as well as dust and dirt, involved in repairing the damage. After several attempts, the exterminator shared the good news that the infested area was clear of termites.

Statistics show that more structures are destroyed by termites than by fire. Termites cause damage behind the scenes. The very structure may deteriorate before anyone is aware of any damage.

Did you know marriages are also destroyed by "termites"? Husbands and wives must continually be on guard and be sensitive to small, seemingly insignificant areas of their lives.

Perhaps the first termite is "Thou hast left thy first love" (Revelation 2:4b). Someone has said, "If we lose something, we can blame it on someone else, but if we leave an item, the person who left the object is directly responsible to again come back to where he left it." Leaving our first love in marriage is also possible. The agape love, the love that comes from God, is our security against unfaithfulness. It is impossible to have a godly relationship with each other if our relationship is not vital and growing. Unless the Bible is closely followed, the secular world and its practices may become the guideline rather than God's holy plan.

Disrespect is another "termite." The vows we made "before God and these witnesses" committed our lives to each other "for better or worse, in sickness or health as long as we both shall live." This promise can be taken far too lightly. Just as termites work in darkness, so many marriages slowly deteriorate. We take each other for granted. We fail to appreciate those little tokens and acts of love. Unkind words are uttered, and actions once considered hurtful are too often the norm. Arguments earlier unthought of are now tolerated. Disrespect becomes the way of life. Courtesy to others outside the family is seemingly more important than showing courtesy to those dearest to us.

A deep spiritual life is missing; therefore, it becomes another "termite" that destroys. It is not likely that a marriage will stand where spiritual values are overlooked. Since God joins two people (Mark 10:9), it is a spiritual relationship. Conflicts and stresses will not break up a marriage where it is held with honor and respect and as a sacred gift from God. The spiritual life provides resources to work through difficulties rather than seeking escape.

Selfishness is another "termite" that destroys. Since man is selfish by nature, self-interest and self-satisfaction is the goal. When two people live together and both live for self, there is bound to be conflict. True godly love motivates a deepening experience in which self dies. Because each is concerned to pursue the joy and security of the other, the success in marriage deepens when the emphasis is placed on God. Self-denial takes the place of self-fulfillment.

Immaturity is also a "termite" that causes confusion and chaos. We must seek God's will and have a proper perspective which comes from a pure heart (Matthew 5:8). Then we will not be plagued with the idea that it has to be done my way, but both are concerned that it is done in God's way for God's glory. God's way always points to Him, to grow up in Him, "speaking the truth in love" (Ephesians 4:15).

Stubbornness is a "termite" that destroys by hindering God's Spirit from working in submitting to each other. Reverence for God and respect for each other is lost when we do not feel the need of help from our spouse. Rather, the attitude is, "I'll do it when and how I want to, when I feel like it."

Another "termite" that destroys under the surface is covetousness. It robs marriage of contentment. There is no peace and joy when there is discontentment. We tend to have the feeling that contentment is found in things rather than the condition of the heart.

Lack of communication can destroy even the best of marriages. Since there is no guesswork in the home, husband and wife should say what they mean and mean what they say. (Back to our termite encounter—when Bennie finally realized the seriousness of the matter, his first response was, "Why didn't you mention it sooner?" I had failed in communicating the urgency of the problem.)

Satan knows that materialism is another subtle "termite." When we over-obligate ourselves, we become too busy to get all the things done that need our attention. We become irritable and impatient with those dearest to us, and often our spiritual life is neglected. I was once challenged that the spiritual status of a person is gauged by the bookmark in their Bible. Does the bookmark move continually, or are we neglecting the most important time of the day? Materialism is usually the cause. In order to keep our material pursuits in proper order, we need to live by Romans 12:1, 2. Also, we must remember to seek God first, then "all these things shall be added unto [us]" (Matthew 6:33).

The temperaments of husband and wife are usually different. Often that is one thing that drew the couple together in courtship, but frequently these differences can become irritations. Instead, we should allow these differences to make us a complete couple.

In Judges 13 there is an interesting account of Manoah and his wife. The angel appeared to his wife first. Then Manoah desired also to hear his message. He was called at the angel's second appearance. Their different responses to the angel are interesting. Manoah impulsively responded, "We shall surely die, because we have seen God" (verse 22). His wife replied more calmly, "If the Lord were pleased to kill us, he would not have received a burnt offering and a meat offering at our hands" (verse 23).

It is God's perfect will that husbands and wives complement each other. At times we may allow a competitive spirit to prevail, which is another "termite." The root problem is jealousy and envy, even though at times we may not be aware of it. We must certainly plead to God to keep our hearts with all diligence (Proverbs 4:23). God's plea is for unity and oneness, not disunity and chaos.

Our tongue is another "termite" that quickly destroys. "But the tongue can no man tame; it is an unruly evil, full of deadly poison. Therewith bless we God, even the Father; and therewith curse we men, which are made after the similitude of God" (James 3:8, 9). Because of our tongue, it is often too easy to blame others for our wrongs and failures. We cannot bless God and at the same time curse or speak evil of each other.

Many of us do not enjoy changes, yet we cannot deny the fact that we are growing older. We will need to change in order to continue living. Growing older makes us take a good look at life in the view of eternity. Resistance to change can be a "termite" that destroys. It need not be a burden to grow older. We do well to recognize this. We cannot live in the springtime of marriage as we enter our mid-life years. To refuse to acknowledge our age is to refuse to accept God's plan. "But though our outward man perish, yet the inward man is renewed day by day" (II Corinthians 4:16).

God's plan is always perfect! He knows if we would retain our youthful looks and ambitions, we would fail to see the seriousness of life and the certainty of eternity. In the godly marriage, it is not the physical beauty and zeal that attracts, "but let it be the hidden man of the heart . . . which is in the sight of God of great price" (I Peter 3:4). That is why it is so important to build our marriage on the agape love, the only love that will stand the test of time and be able to exterminate the "termites."

God's Will for You and Me

*Just to be tender, just to be true
Just to be glad, the whole day through!
Just to be merciful, just to be mild
Just to be trustful, as a child
Just to be gentle and kind and sweet
Just to be helpful with willing feet
Just to be cheery, when things go wrong
Just to drive sadness away with a song.*

*Whether the hour is dark or bright
Just to be loyal to God and right.
Just to believe, God knows best
Just in His promises ever to rest
Just to let love be our daily key
That is God's will for you and me.*

"*. . . and serve him with a perfect heart and with a willing mind: for the Lord searcheth all hearts, and understandeth all the imaginations of the thoughts: if thou seek him, he will be found of thee . . .*" (I Chronicles 28:9).

—*Author unknown*

16

God's Perfect or Permissive Will

"Set thine house in order; for thou shalt die and not live," was the message the Prophet Isaiah brought to King Hezekiah (II Kings 20:1b).

I wonder how a message such as this would affect me. (Although we are all aware that we, too, need continually to set our house in order because we know not how much time God has allotted to us.)

King Hezekiah responded by turning his face to the wall and begging God. He said, "O Lord, remember how I walked before thee in truth and with a perfect heart, and have done that which is good in thy sight" (II Kings 20:3). Then he wept sore.

God must have changed his mind, because He spoke to Isaiah before he left the court. God sent Isaiah back to King Hezekiah with another message. God said, "I have heard thy prayer . . . behold, I will heal thee . . . I will add unto thy days fifteen years" (II Kings 20:5, 6a).

God's perfect or permissive will comes to my mind as I read this account of King Hezekiah.

During these fifteen years that God added to the king's life, a son, Manasseh, was born. He began his reign at the age of twelve, after his father's death. All through II Kings, Chapter 21, we find the evil deeds of King Manasseh.

More blood was shed during his reign than during any other king's reign. He built altars to idols and even made his sons pass through the fire (II Kings 21:6). Much wickedness was the result of King Hezekiah's desire for God's permissive will rather than God's perfect will.

What is our position? Are we satisfied and happy with God's perfect will, or do we plead to God and turn our face to the wall and weep sore?

At his conversion, the Apostle Paul was struck down by a bright light. His question was, "Lord, what wilt thou have me to do?" (Acts 9:5, 6). This is the important question. It is still the result of a person who is seeking God's perfect will. Paul thought he was doing God's will when he "[breathed] out threatenings and slaughter against the disciples of the Lord . . ." (Acts 9:1). But when he came face to face with Jesus, he wanted to know what Jesus' will was for him.

George Mueller's life gives testimony to the perfect will of God. His simple faith in God was an amazement to the whole world in his day. Someone once asked him what his formula was in determining God's divine will, to which he replied, "I seek at the beginning to get my heart into such a state that it has no will of its own in regard to a given matter." Most of the difficulties are overcome when our hearts are ready to do the Lord's will.

Since Paul was obedient to God in faithfully following through with God's perfect will, he gives us a blueprint by which we also are able to find God's perfect will. "I [beg] you therefore, brethren, by the mercies of God, that ye present your bodies a living sacrifice, holy, acceptable unto God, which is your reasonable service. And be not conformed to this world; but be ye transformed by the renewing of your mind, that ye may prove what is that good, and acceptable, and perfect, will of God" (Romans 12:1, 2). How wonderful that our heavenly Father gives us precise instructions on how we can find and follow His perfect will!

STEP ONE: "Present your bodies a living sacrifice." This means utter, unreserved undivided surrender. Often it is in this first step that we fail to follow God's blueprint, and this is why there is so much confusion and unrest in the hearts and lives of Christians today. When I surrender my body as a living sacrifice it means, "I am crucified with Christ: nevertheless I live; yet not I, but Christ liveth in me" (Galatians 2:20). I claim no rights for myself, but I find in Jesus my all in all.

STEP TWO: "And be not conformed to this world." The world's pattern of life is one of selfishness, sinfulness, materialism, greed, and lust. We are living in a "me first" society. Eyes are blinded to spiritual realities and objectives; therefore, the will of God cannot be perceived. We must pay the price of separation. It costs our whole life, and all our motives and actions. We must walk in the light and knowledge of God's Word. Then there will be power to live victoriously, to be well-pleasing to God, and to be approved of men (Romans 14:18).

STEP THREE: "Be ye transformed by the renewing of your mind." This is only our reasonable service.

Our minds, our spirits, and our entire spiritual lives must constantly be refreshed by dwelling in Christ's presence and feeding on His Word. Unless this is our frame of mind, the perfect will of God cannot be found. A carnal-minded person cannot please God (Romans 8:8).

The whole course of life must be spiritual, a daily, constant walk with God through prayer and reading His Word. This is the only way our lives will be renewed, refreshed, and transformed so that God can bless us with the knowledge of His Will.

Why settle for less than God's best? We know that God is pleased when we obediently and joyfully follow Him. With such an attitude, we find joy in fulfilling our tasks. We toil and labor long and hard for the sake of God and our families, as a wife and mother. Those seemingly undesirable tasks become meaningful when we do them as unto the Lord (Colossians 3:17). It is then that we will be able to face those hard, unexpected, and frustrating times which are bound to come to all of us. As we daily walk in His presence and live in His fellowship, we will not need to rush to God and ask for a quick answer at an unexpected frustration, or when an emergency arises. We will find we can experience what the prophet says in Isaiah 30:21, "Thine ears shall hear a [voice] behind thee saying, This is the way, walk ye in it, when ye turn to the right hand, and when ye turn to the left."

It is in loving,
        not in being loved
The heart finds its quest;
It is in giving,
        not in getting
Our lives are blessed.

A Family Prayer

Dear God in heaven, help us to make our home a happy place . . . an orderly home of love, peace, and contentment . . . a place of work and worship . . . where You are always the center and where people known and unknown are always welcome.

Through the passing years, keep us faithful to Thee and loyal to each other, always keeping within that blessed realm of Your hedge of protection until we reach our eternal home in heaven.

In Jesus' name,
Amen

17

Love Without a "Net"

"... Will you love and cherish, in health and in sickness, in prosperity and in adversity, share the joys and sorrows of life, exercising patience, kindness, and forbearance, live in peace as becometh a faithful Christian couple, forsaking all others, keep yourselves only for each other as long as you both shall live?"

Not one of us who has made those vows had any idea what all would be included when we answered, "I will." But we need not worry or be anxious because "I know whom I have believed and am persuaded that [God] is able to keep that which I have committed unto him against that day" (II Timothy 1:12).

When we love without a "net" or stipulation, we free our spouse and our children to become all that God has planned for them to become. For some, this means we must say "yes" to more responsibilities than raising our family or being a supportive church member. To some, this comes early in married life. We must let go and allow God to have our husbands lead the church. Often God does not wait until we feel we are willing, neither does God wait until the children are grown. Therefore, it weighs heavily upon the wife to carry added responsibility in teaching and caring for the family in order to free the husband to do God's bidding.

We dare not entertain thoughts such as "I have been neglected" or "My needs are unmet." This would be the

91

first step in squelching my husband's effectiveness. Attitudes such as these are likened to a net used to catch prized butterflies. All the fluttering is to no avail! But allow the butterfly liberty, and it beautifies the surrounding area. That is how it is in our homes when we allow God to have full control of our husband's and our children's lives. It blesses and enlarges our capacity to appreciate and enjoy God's vast areas of service, and it brings "joy unspeakable and full of glory" (I Peter 1:8).

Murmurings and complainings are another "net" that will hinder our effectiveness.

At times I am tempted to think it has been a long time since I had my husband's *unhurried* attention. Then I recognize that my husband belongs to God first of all. This helps me to find joy and fulfillment in knowing God comes first, and since "I am crucified with Christ: nevertheless I live; yet not I, but Christ liveth in me" (Galatians 2:20), then I will not feel slighted or neglected if God's work takes my husband's or my children's time.

If I have no rights of my own, then I have nothing to lose or complain about. Someone has wisely said, "It is much better to have 10 percent of a 100 percent man, than to have 100 percent of a 10 percent man." This helps me keep my priorities straight.

Charles Spurgeon is known as one of the greatest eighteenth century evangelists. He was married to Susanna Thompson, a dedicated young woman who was a good example of one who "loved without a net." Charles kept a very busy schedule of speaking engagements around London and throughout the British Isles.

Once when Charles was preparing to leave for another series of meetings, she broke into tears. She did not want him to leave. He had an interesting response: "Susie, do you think when the Israelites brought a lamb as an offering to the Lord they stood and wept over it?" She shook her head, to which he replied, "Well, don't you see that you are giving me to God as your sacrifice in letting me go and preach the Gospel? Do you think God wants you to cry over your sacrifice?"

Perhaps some of us wives of busy husbands can also identify with Susie Spurgeon. But we must be challenged that we need not weep over what we think is a sacrifice.

It is often true that in marriage opposite temperaments attract each other; this gives much room and many opportunities to grow and to expand our capacities.

Charles was known to be a straightforward, uneducated fellow with a "countrified" manner, and his speech often brought more embarrassment than reverence. Susie was just the opposite. She was the daughter of a prosperous merchant. She was proper and reserved, yet it was her dedicated spiritual life that won Charles' heart.

Charles' zeal for God's Word and his burden for God's people, and Susie's educated, pious, "proper" Christian life was the combination that God needed to make Charles Spurgeon the outstanding preacher he was.

Susie could have demanded more of Charles' time and attention, but because of her deep devotion to her Lord and Saviour, she encouraged her husband to be all that God wanted him to be. She did not confine him to a "net"!

The same was true in Charles' life. Since he was an uneducated, countrified preacher, he was blessed by Susie's ability to read Greek and Hebrew. She often assisted him in his message preparation.

Susie was a good mother to their twin boys. Since her husband was a busy man, much of the teaching and training was left for Susie to do. In all this, both of the boys grew up also to serve in the ministry in later years.

Not only was Susie an assistance to Charles' ministry, but she also founded a book fund in which she distributed thousands of books to others. Many of these were copies of Charles' messages.

Charles not only loved his wife and gave her credit for helping his ministry become successful, but he also encouraged her to find fulfillment in becoming all God wanted her to become.

David Livingston once asked Charles, "How do you manage to do two days' work in a single day?" Charles replied without hesitation, "You forgot there are two of us. My wife and I, we work together."[1] What a challenge! In loving without a net, much can be accomplished when "love comes from a pure heart" (I Timothy 1:5).

It has been said that fishermen who harvest crabs need never fear losing any crabs once they are netted and placed in a container. They keep each other from escaping! When one begins to climb out of the container, its peers are there to pull it down.

Let it not be once said of us as husbands and wives that our spouse or our children are not free to become all God wants them to become, to rise to levels of maturity, because we are guilty of the "crab treatment."

Loving without a "net" is described as "putting aside the past, doing our best while living in each day, and earnestly pressing toward the goal of conforming to the image of our Lord and Saviour" (Philippians 3:13, 14, paraphrased).

---

1. William J. Petersen, *Catherine Marshall Had a Husband* (Wheaton, Illinois: Tyndale House Publishers, 1986), pp. 121-156.

I used to pray that God would do this or that. Now I pray that God will make His will known to me.

—Mme. Chiang Kai-shek

Abide in Me

Dear child of my love, why worry and fret
  About things that you must do.
It is "Dying" not "Doing" that bringeth forth fruit.
  And all that I want is "Just YOU."
It's the Life of the tree that flows through the branch.
  That produces the fruit that you see.
And the fruits of the Spirit shall surely be seen.
  If you'll just keep "Abiding in Me."

Does the branch ever struggle and try to bear fruit.
  How vain all its efforts would be.
The purpose for which it was formed is attained
  As it stays in its place on the tree.
And the small grain of wheat must fall into the ground
  And die, e'er ever new life shall appear.
By its dying, alone comes "Abundance of Life"
  First the blade, then full corn in the Ear.

The Beautiful Rose, and the Lily, so fair,
  Never worry, or fret, they "just grow."
From whence comes their Beauty, their Fragrance, so sweet
  Only He, who created them knows.
And to Him who redeemed thee, most precious thou art
  Like a bright shining light, thou shalt be.
With His "Life more Abundant," and such "Fulness of Joy,"
  All thy friends shall see Jesus, in thee.

Courtesy of Baxter Lane Company, Armarillo, TX, 1975
Used by permission.

18

Prepare for the Rainy Day

To many women, rainy days are depressing, but consider the opposite condition—the pressing heat, the dry and brown countryside, the barren and bleak surroundings. We would live in a desert!

Rainy days are a blessing from God. How relaxing to watch a gentle rain, to notice black clouds gathering, and to hear the welcome sound of thunder. Observe the grandeur of lightning, and suddenly feel the cool, refreshing breeze of an abrupt downpour. Then discover a beautiful rainbow shortly afterwards.

God never forgets His children. Just as He placed a rainbow in the sky to remind Noah of His promise (Genesis 9:13), so the rainbow is still a sign of God's promise that He will never leave nor forsake us (Hebrews 13:5b).

Just as nature needs rain, so we need rainy days to perfect and refresh our spiritual lives.

First of all, we need to maintain a vital personal relationship with our Creator. Our lives must be in order: sins confessed up-to-date and encouragement given when there is opportunity. Then with confidence in God, we can meet the not-so-pleasant experiences in life and acknowledge them as sent from God.

An elderly saint has been a continual inspiration to me. He always has a word of encouragement for everyone. His countenance is always cheerful. When I asked him what his secret was, he replied, "I have never a met a disappointment, because years ago, I placed a capital *H* where the *d* is in *disappointment*. He further said, "A person can live such a life that as he grows older and looks back, he will have few, if any regrets." He had learned by God's grace to obey God promptly, quickly, and cheerfully. "Hear counsel, and receive instruction, that thou mayest be wise in thy latter end. There are many devices in a man's heart; nevertheless the counsel of the Lord, that shall stand" (Proverbs 19:20, 21).

Since thanksgiving and murmuring are not found in the same heart, we must decide how we are going to face life. Either we grumble and complain because self is on the throne and is never satisfied, or we will, through thanksgiving and praise, be so busy serving our Master and others that we have no time to lament and complain about that which we don't have.

Guy Doud shares how he prepared for the rainy day. He and his dad had a good father-son relationship, often encouraging each other and sharing their hopes and ambitions. After one such memorable evening, they parted, little realizing this was their last conversation. Several days later, a phone call alerted Guy that his dad had suffered a massive heart attack. When Guy and his friend entered the embalming room, Joe asked Guy if there was anything he would have liked to tell his dad. With deep respect, Guy said he could think of nothing that he needed to talk to his dad about. "Everything I ever wanted to tell him I did." Their communication was up-to-date! They were both prepared for the rainy day.[1]

During the 1989 earthquake in San Francisco, California, a certain lady was home schooling her daughter. The mother gave her daughter the assignments and then hurried to the grocery store. The little girl was tempted to leave her books and play with her cat but decided to obey

---

1. Guy Rice Doud, *Molder of Dreams* (Pomona, California: Focus on the Family Publishing, 1990), pp. 46-47.

her mother instead. Suddenly, the earth quaked, crashing the chimney of the house and killing the family cat. What a blessing obedience proved to be! If the daughter had disobeyed, she may have died along with the cat. But through obedience, mother and daughter were both blessed and prepared for the rainy day.

Sleepless nights can perhaps be classed as rainy days. These nights need not be filled with frustrations and murmurings, because God wants us to meditate on Him day and night. "His delight is in the law of the Lord; and in his law doth he meditate day and night" (Psalm 1:2). At times during the night we may feel prompted to pray for someone who is in a difficult or dangerous situation. Our families need intercessory prayer. The aged, our youth, the church, and our government may all be blessed by our prayers. Try praying for each church family and each family member. It is much better to talk to the Great Shepherd than to count sheep!

As we grow older, we experience aches and pains unknown to the younger person. It is up to each one of us whether we allow the rainy days to make us better or bitter. For both husbands and wives, it is important to have a scheduled lifestyle. But, in spite of this, we will need to be flexible because it is God who orders our steps as well as our stops.

God told King Hezekiah, "Set thine house in order; for thou shalt die, and not live" (II Kings 20:1). God's call to parents today is to keep our homes in order, for we know not what the day may hold. For "there is but a step between me and death" (I Samuel 20:3b).

We as homemakers and wives do our families a favor by planning and keeping our housework up-to-date if at all possible: clean when there is a need; can and freeze when the produce is ready; keep the laundry and mending done; in the evening, organize the house, making it neat and livable; be sensitive to the family's needs; fix the broken toy; mend a broken heart.

Always keep in mind that the words you speak may be the last words you will utter.

Teach the children at every opportunity, because we dare not put off for tomorrow what must be done today. Second Peter 3:14 tells us what kind of person God requires: ". . . be diligent that ye may be found of him in peace, without spot, and blameless."

We need not dread or fear the rainy days in life. If we walk with Jesus in the sunshine, He will walk with us through the rainy days!

God's Word must first enter the mind,
before it can enter the heart.

Don't Quit

When things go wrong, as they sometimes will,
When the road you're trudging seems all up hill,
When the funds are low and the debts are high,
And you want to smile, but you have to sigh,
When care is pressing you down a bit,
Rest, if you must—but don't you quit,
Life is queer with its twists and turns,
As everyone of us sometimes learns,
And many a failure turns about
When he might have won had he stuck it out;
Don't give up, though the pace seems slow—
You may succeed with another blow.
Success is failure turned inside out—
The silver tint of the clouds of doubt
And you never can tell just how close you are,
It may be near when it seems afar;
So stick to the fight when you're hardest hit—
It's when things seem worst that you mustn't quit.

Courtesy of Baxter Lane Company, Armarillo, TX, 1975.
Used by permission.

19

Finding the Solution

Oil on the garage floor again! It had become a daily ordeal to clean up the oil by pouring gasoline on the area and wiping it up with paper towels. But the question remained, Where is the oil coming from? A trip to the mechanic indicated that the car needed a new head gasket. The problem had been solved, the question answered, but there was a price to pay.

Two different accounts in the Bible come to my mind as I think of paying the price to find the solution.

One is in II Samuel 24. The Bible tells us that David sinned by numbering the people. When David was convicted of this sin, he confessed to God, "Lo, I have sinned, and I have done wickedly" (verse 17). He was willing to do what God required, and he paid the price to find the solution.

The second account is found in I Kings 13. King Jeroboam became angry when the "man of God" pointed out his sin. As the king stretched out his hand and pointed his finger, his hand "dried up, so that he could not pull it in again to him" (verse 4b). Then in verse 6, King Jeroboam entreated the prophet to seek God and pray for his restoration. God answered the prophet's prayer.

Instead of repenting and paying for the solution, he invited the prophet to come to his house. The king wanted to show the prophet kindness by giving him gifts. King Jeroboam was satisfied to continue "cleaning up the spot of oil" rather than the sin of his rebellious heart. Not so with King David. He harkened to the prophet and followed his instructions precisely. David went to Araunah's threshing floor and asked to buy the place to build an altar to make a sacrifice there to God. In the kindness of Araunah's heart, he offered to give King David the place, the oxen, and even the threshing instruments and other instruments for wood for the offering. (See II Kings 24, verses 21 and 22).

David's answer in verse 24 is a challenge, "Nay; but I will surely buy it of thee for a price: neither will I offer burnt offerings unto the Lord my God of that which doth cost me nothing." No wonder David is called a man after God's own heart (I Samuel 13:14 and Acts 13:22). When there was sin and failure, he repented and obeyed God wholeheartedly. He refused to sacrifice anything that did not cost him. He found the solution!

In which category do we find ourselves? It is easy to brush over some unkind or harsh remark with the idea that I'll just be careful what I say next time, or I'll do some extra work to amend a broken or hurting relationship. Perhaps even a bouquet of flowers attempt to say what words should say, but don't.

In the past two weeks I faced two different encounters that required repentance and restitution. Once it was a phone call to acknowledge a statement that I had made that could have hindered God's working in the life of an individual. The second one was provoking a family member to anger. I was deeply convicted both times, and after confession my heart felt so clean and free. Each time there was a price to pay and no amount of "nice kindness" could undo those faults or sins.

We do need to allow our spouse and children the freedom to make mistakes, but we need to continually be seeking for the solution. By applying God's Word, we will not be making the same mistake time and again.

We should be challenged to grow in our Christian

experience. As we grow, the Holy Spirit will minister grace and strength to us in finding the solution, and not just being content to occasionally clean up the oil. In Luke 22:43, the angels ministered to Jesus' need when He faced the Calvary experience. He was strengthened, and He was victorious. Therefore, He is our example of victory in everything.

In Jesus is found the price for our victory, and in Jesus we find the solution!

What God Has Given Me

I haven't a mansion, title, or wealth
  But I have my family and good health
I have the sun and the sky so blue
  And lots of good neighbors, too.
I have the moon and the stars so bright
  To light up the sky in the darkest night
I haven't a yacht to sail on the sea
  But I have a husband who loves only me.
So I thank God in heaven above
  For giving me these things to love.

—*Author unknown*

20

Living in the Basement

Our visitors had just arrived. As they stepped inside the door, they took a quick survey and exclaimed, "So you live in the basement!"

Did you know that many people live in the basement in a spiritual sense?

It has been said that a person is like a three-story building with a top story, first floor, and the basement. The top story is the spiritual nature, the first floor is the mental nature, and the basement is the selfish or fleshly nature. Many people use their mental nature to feed their selfish nature, while their spiritual nature starves.

To be a well-adjusted, balanced person, one must develop the whole person. Overdevelop your selfish, lower nature, and you will become even more selfish and ingrown. Overdevelop your mental nature to the exclusion of the spiritual and you will become a skeptic. Few, if any, overdevelop the spiritual nature, for that is hard to do. But if you pay due attention to your spiritual nature, you will give proper attention to your mental and physical well-being as well. Luke 2:52 states that "Jesus increased in wisdom and stature, and in favor with God and man." In this verse, the fourfold nature of man is indicated regarding our Lord. *Wisdom* refers to the mind, *stature* to the body, *favor with God* to the spiritual, and *man* to the social.

"Study to shew thyself approved unto God, a workman that needeth not to be ashamed, rightly dividing the word of truth" (II Timothy 2:15).

Confirming our guest's exclamation, we do live in the basement of our house! It is a large, pleasant room. In one corner is a well-supplied kitchen, where many meals have been prepared and served from a beautiful cherry dining room table. On the opposite side of the room is the sewing nook, where the family sewing is done. Also built into this cabinet is the stereo music system—though out of view, it can be enjoyed by all. To the right is a fireplace and a large family room which is carpeted, cozy, and homey. The sun shines through the double windows most of the day, causing the atmosphere to be pleasant and bright. Effort must be taken to view the neighbors or the busy highway, because there are no windows except toward the woods.

I love living in the basement of our house. It is a place where our family and friends are always welcome. Here we close the door to the outside world. It is cool and comfortable in the summer and pleasantly cozy in the winter. But as much as I love our basement quarters, I am deeply concerned to live well above the basement level spiritually.

You have probably heard these statements: "Tell me what kind of books or papers you read and I will tell you what kind of person you are," or "Let me see your bookshelves and magazine racks because that tells volumes about the family who occupies the house."

Many husbands and wives feed on unwholesome magazines, novels, or sensual sex stories and find themselves becoming discontented with their marriages and homes. To them, the Christian home fails to have the glitter and glamour that appears in their reading world.

For Christians, this should be totally out of thinking to stoop to such reading and waste God's precious time on such trash. To do so grieves the blessed Holy Spirit. Persons who read such unwholesome material become lean in their souls; worse than that, they are backsliding.

Jeremiah 10:20, 21 gives a picture of such a home. "My tabernacle is spoiled, and all my cords are broken: my children are gone forth of me, and they are not.... For the [parents] are become brutish, and have not sought the Lord: therefore they shall not prosper, and all their [families] shall be scattered."

But since God is a great and wonderful God and "not willing that any should perish" (II Peter 3:9), He gives us the remedy. If we see "the exceeding sinfulness of sin" (Romans 7:13), we get a glimpse of His holiness and we will turn to God for forgiveness. He is always there.

"O Lord, I know that the way of man is not in himself: it is not in man . . . to direct his steps. O Lord, correct me, but with judgment . . ." (Jeremiah 10:23, 24). "But put ye on the Lord Jesus Christ, and make not provision for the flesh, to fulfill the lusts thereof" (Romans 13:14). As the proper steps are taken to confess and to forsake our sin, God's grace will pardon abundantly. There will be a hunger and thirst for God's Word and God's will.

Dismiss from your mind the idea that the Bible is a dry, uninteresting book. Such an attitude betrays the fact that you are not becoming acquainted with God's divine and holy Word.

Ask God to enlighten your mind as you read. Make practical application to everyday living, and you will be blessed to find how rich God's Word is and how satisfying to your weary, longing soul.

Yes, God's Word is yours as you read and use it. There is no need to live in the basement spiritually.

Rules for Daily Life

BEGIN THE DAY WITH GOD;
     Kneel down to Him in prayer;
Lift up thy heart to His abode.
     And seek His love to share.

OPEN THE BOOK OF GOD,
     And read a portion there;
That it may hallow all thy thoughts,
     And sweeten all thy care.

GO THROUGH THE DAY WITH GOD,
     Whate'er thy work may be;
Where'er thou art—at home, abroad,
     He still is near to thee.

CONVERSE IN MIND WITH GOD,
     Thy spirit heavenward raise:
Acknowledge every good bestowed,
     And offer grateful praise.

CONCLUDE THE DAY WITH GOD,
     Thy sins to Him confess;
Trust in the Lord's atoning blood,
     And plead His righteousness.

LIE DOWN AT NIGHT WITH GOD.
     Who gives His servants sleep;
And when thou tread'st the vale of death,
     He will thee guard and keep.

Courtesy of Baxter Lane Company, Armarillo, TX, 1975.
Used by permission.

21

Walk the Chalk Line!

On the way home from church, my mom informed us that Pete and Sara had invited our family to share the following Sunday dinner with them. What excitement and anticipation for our family of four eager children, who always thought it to be very special when we had an invitation to dinner, and especially to Pete and Sara's house!

Our anticipation soared as Sunday approached. On the way, my wise dad looked at his four children in the back seat of our horse-drawn carriage. With sternness in his voice, Dad said, "Children, you walk the chalk line today! Sit still and don't ask for toys, and speak softly when you are spoken to. When we are sitting at the table, eat with your mouth closed, take only one serving, and be sure to eat all your food. Now, remember your manners," my dad added.

Pete and Sara didn't have any children, so their house was always immaculate. No wonder Dad needed to give us these instructions since we were a lively group of children.

In my growing-up years, I was often reminded to "walk the chalk line." Even though it took me years to really appreciate my dad's advice, I am thankful I learned it years ago. God also measured His people with a straight-edge.

A chalk line is a valuable tool in the hand of a builder. He often uses it to give direction in order to nail two pieces of material together. *Chalk up,* according to Webster, means "to attain or to achieve."

This is what my dad had in mind when he told me to "walk the chalk line." A good illustration of this is found in Romans 3:20-21 (Philips): ". . . indeed it is the straightedge of the law that shows us how crooked we are."[1]

The Bible also speaks of a plumb line. This is a cord with a weight on one end which serves to determine the vertical point of an object. "Therefore thus saith the Lord; I am returned to Jerusalem with mercies: my house shall be built in it . . . and a line shall be stretched forth upon Jerusalem" (Zechariah 1:16). Also in Amos 7:8, ". . . the Lord said unto me, Amos, what seest thou? And I said, A plumbline. Then said the Lord, Behold, I will set a plumbline in the midst of my people Israel." The Greek root word for *plumbline* is "to be narrow." Could it mean a narrow course on which to walk?

Needless to say, "walking the chalk line" is still part of my life. I have often been thankful for a strict dad who insisted that we walk straight and who also took strong measures if we disobeyed.

Seemingly, some builders today have the idea that the chalk line isn't as important as it was years ago. Could it be possible that the chalk line has lost its significance in the home; therefore, we fail to instill this important aspect in our children's lives?

A disciplined life can be viewed as walking the chalk line. It is described as training that corrects, molds, and perfects the moral character of a person. A disciplined person has a godly perspective, with a vision of much work to be done; therefore, there is no time for boredom. The mind is alert and curious to the extent that the person wants to learn all he can in his short life span, to become

---

1. J. B. Philips, *New Testament in Modern English* (New York: MacMillian Company, 1957).

all God has planned. When there is time on hand, a disciplined person will not be at a loss to know what to do but adapts easily to people or solitude. No one is needed to entertain such a person.

In order to parent disciplined children, we must first be disciplined ourselves. I claim *no* right to myself, but God is my whole portion. Since more is caught than taught in the disciplined life, it is of great importance that we exemplify by our life what we would desire in the lives of our children.

First of all, a disciplined life comes from loving God with all our heart, soul, and mind, then our neighbor as ourselves (Matthew 22:37). Obedience follows love closely. Someone has wisely said, "Prompt obedience is the only obedience that God counts. Slow obedience is no obedience."

Compassion and servitude are the attitudes of a disciplined heart, first to God in sincere thanksgiving and praise, and then to others all around who will also be loved, appreciated, encouraged, and blessed.

Contentment, too, is a virtue—not content with who we are but content with God's will for our lives. Cheerfulness and gratitude are two more qualities that prevail in a disciplined life. With these qualities, our speech and way of life will witness of our Christianity.

We will also be moderate. We will live within reasonable limits, and calmness and temperance will express our life. In all that we do, we must live consistently in order to insist that our children "walk the chalk line."

We are certainly living in a day of blurred lines and nondescript grays. In the modern mind, nearly anything is acceptable. We are shocked by the gross immorality around us, but let us not forget that much of this is the result of gradual erosion of the disciplined life. If we want good fruit, we must feed the roots. We cannot separate Christian discipline from the reverence and worship that pleases God.

The challenge to me is, if I want my children to walk the chalk line, I must have convictions that show the way of God's chalk line, in God's way, for God's glory.

Obedience is the acid test of a disciplined life. Gold is not changed by a drop of acid, but gold is refined and polished when acid is applied. All other metals either change or corrode. The same is true for the Christian: if he is not gold, he will not be able to "walk God's chalk line."

Anything done without heart,
is done in the dark!

Kitchen Prayer

Bless my little kitchen, Lord
And light it with Thy Love.
Help me plan and make my meals
From Thy heavenly home above.
Bless our meals with Thy Presence
And warm them with Thy grace;
Watch over me as I do my work,
Washing pots and pans and plates.
The service I am trying to do
Is to make my family content,
So bless my eager efforts, Lord
And make them heaven sent.

Courtesy of Baxter Lane Company, Armarillo, TX, 1975.
Used by permission.

22

Gather Up the Fragments

Here in America, we cut a loaf of bread into neat, uniform pieces. But in Central America and in other countries, people break bits off a loaf of bread or cake. I suppose this is how it was done in Palestine when Jesus broke the bread and blessed it and fed the multitude. It was broken pieces, not slices or leftovers.

What a comfort and encouragement to read the account in John 6. Jesus not only blessed the bread, but He broke it and shared with the people. Therefore, every morsel He had blessed was, in His sight, worth gathering up for later use!

Do we at times feel like odds and ends of loaves, not worthy to be called anything? We need not despair. As we become broken pieces that He can bless, then our lives will be useful. Even the "crumbs" of our lives will not be lost. If my life is broken when given to Jesus, it will become pieces that will feed many, while a loaf will satisfy only one. A similar account of the five loaves and two fishes is also found in Luke 9:14-17. It is of interest that both St. John and St. Luke must have been impressed with Jesus' miracle, and both were inspired to relate the account.

Zechariah 4:10 tells us not to "[despise] the day of small things." Later in the verse he gives the reason. We dare not overlook small things, because "the eyes of the Lord . . . run to and fro through the whole earth." If it was important in Zechariah's day, how much more in our day.

God's eye does behold everything! It is so important to be sensitive to little things, that nothing be lost.

It was a typical Sunday morning. The rest of the family was in the car, ready to go to church. As usual, I waited until everyone else went outside, then I made my round to see that the time bake was turned on the proper temperature. I turned off a light, switched the fan on low, and pushed the doorknob to lock the door. A quick glance around the kitchen reminded me that someone had left their Bible on the table, and the Amish Mennonite Aid newsletters were left on the sewing machine cabinet. My arms were full of various items that needed to be taken along to church that specific morning. As I took my place in the front seat of the car, one of the girls said, "Mom gathered up the fragments." As I pondered the statement, I was challenged anew that as mothers we are often called upon to gather up the pieces. We are to work behind the scenes to keep the household organized and keep things ticking.

In the day of modern conveniences, it is very easy to throw away little things. Rather than repairing the electric range because the timer wears out, we lightly toss it aside and buy a new one. After all, it's fifteen years old. Perhaps Mr. Jones would really be glad for it. He probably wouldn't even use the timer. The hoe or shovel handle is broken and, we reason, it takes too long to chisel out the old handle and replace it with a new one. We'll just buy a brand-new one instead. The lawn mower just isn't fast enough, so I become discontented wishing for a better mower rather than enjoying walking more slowly and beholding the beauty of a freshly mowed lawn. A glance in the refrigerator reminds me that there are leftovers that need to be used, but instead, I would rather fix a meal from fresh foods. So out the door goes enough to feed a hungry child in a war-torn country. We should not throw out, but repair where we can, and fix food from our abundance. We need to acknowledge that our overabundance at times makes us despise little, insignificant things.

We often lose little opportunities to teach our children by example that we are stewards of God's many blessings and that "the Lord is in his holy temple . . . his eyes behold, his eyelids try, the children of men" (Psalm 11:4). Let us take the challenge to teach our children the blessing of contentment and the blessing of making good use of little things. Our husbands also need encouragement to be sensitive to save and be a good steward of the many blessings God has entrusted us with. God does not measure us by success but by faithfulness in little things. There is a real blessing and fulfillment in being a mother who is willing to "gather up the fragments that remain, that nothing be lost" (John 6:12).

The Joys of a Mother

I've done an angel's work today!
Yes, such an honor came my way.
Real angel's work! And, lest you doubt it,
I'm going to tell you all about it.
Well, first I cooked. It was so nice
To plan the pies, stewed fruit, and rice.
God sent his angel once to make
Cakes for a poor wayfarer's sake.
But, just today He honored me,
And sent the task my way, you see.
Then, while I tidied up the place,
Gave every knob a radiant face,
Back of my mind this thought would lurk,
That I was still at angel's work.
Putting away coats and dresses,
And moving small unsightliness.
For, oh! 'tis such a lovesome thing,
Just straightening out and freshening.
And after that I washed a few
Small woolly garments, old, not new,
Things I had rubbed and rinsed before
Quite forty times, or even more.
And as I hung them on the line
I thought what God-like work was mine!
To cleanse—ah, me! to wash out stains
Till not a single speck remains.
So, later in the day 'twas sweet
To sit and rest my tired feet
Mending the clothes, and plan out, too,
How to make old things into new.
For surely 'tis an angel's way
To put things right from day to day,
To find thin places, and repair
The glad rags and the sturdy wear.
Since wear and tear must surely be
On this side of Eternity,
I'm feeling very blessed to say
I've done an angel's work today!

—*Author unknown*

Courtesy of Sword of the Lord Publishers, Murfresboro, TN, 1969.
Used by permission.

23

The Joy of Housecleaning

Homemaking is said to be a biblical lifestyle and a joy to the Christian wife and mother. It is within this realm that she finds joy in housecleaning!

Webster describes *joy* as "expressing delight, feeling successful." I believe every wife does find a bit of pleasure when she has accomplished the task of cleaning house.

Proverbs 24:3, 4 gives us a picture of a clean, God-fearing home. "Through wisdom is an house builded; and by understanding it is established: And by knowledge shall the chambers be filled with all precious and pleasant riches." Since "the fear of the Lord is the beginning of knowledge" (Proverbs 1:7), the home must be built on godly principles. *Understanding* is a much-needed ingredient in the home (Proverbs 4:7). This indicates prudence, insight, and intelligence. *Knowledge* is gained through the senses; therefore, God's principles are in circulation. Only then can the rooms be filled with precious memories. Moments are temporary, but memories last a lifetime. There is something inviting, warm, and endearing about such a home. It need not be immaculate, but modestly clean. With small children, the house will not stay perfectly in order, but it can still be clean even though toys clutter the floor.

I have often been grateful for a mother who could organize. She taught her three girls to get work done, even though many times I pushed things into corners or tried to hide unpleasant tasks. But when I got married, I knew it depended on me to get my work done. I didn't have much time to debate whether I wanted to or whether it was necessary. I knew I must do my work or suffer the consequences of an untidy home.

Many choices must be made daily, and often people are tempted to think, "I don't like to do the cleaning so I'll do it later." But we have no promise of tomorrow! "Whereas ye know not what shall be on the morrow" (James 4:14a). It is always a good policy to do the cleaning or other jobs promptly, without procrastinating.

I have learned the joy of housecleaning, but I am indebted to Ella May Miller, speaker on the former *Heart to Heart* broadcast and author of many books for homemakers, whose interesting and noble writings encouraged me to put God first, my family next, and to give them all I have. Many of her thoughts, quotes, and writings have molded my thinking and lifestyle to become all God planned for our family. I am deeply grateful to God and Ella May. It is for this reason I want to encourage all wives, and especially young wives, of the importance of living with a purpose and zeal even in the so-called "lowly" tasks of housecleaning.

When our first waking thoughts are of God, it can be with gratitude to our heavenly Father that we can "rise and shine"! Perhaps a phrase of song comes to mind, or during the warm season it is often the song of the whippoor-will that alerts me to the beginning of a brand-new day. Dressing with a neat and clean appearance can be pleasantly attractive to our families.

The first room that should be kept pleasantly clean and attractive should be the bedroom. Make the bed wrinkle-free, straighten up the room so everything is in place, then close the door.

It should be our privilege to spend some time in Bible reading and prayer, if not first thing in the morning, perhaps a later time would suit better. We should also be concerned that our husbands and children have a nutritious breakfast and family worship before the family go their various ways. After breakfast, the kitchen should be cleaned up: dishes washed and put into the cabinet; the counters, stove, and refrigerator clean and in order.

Many women find it important to write down goals that they would like to achieve for a day or a week. It's a good policy to get the unpleasant tasks done first. Try timing yourself, then set goals, and you will be surprised and blessed to find the tasks were not so dreadful, neither did time slip away from you. The slogan "Work well planned is work half done" is very true! Some spend so much time planning and talking about how they want to perform that they find no time left for their performance.

Another room that can be kept pleasant and clean is the living room. A wife feels much better about herself (and I think this is a part of joy) if there is organization in the living room, when it is kept orderly for family and guests alike. If it is possible, the living room door could be closed. Children will soon know where the limits are. But mothers must be consistent; they dare not demand the door to be closed one day and then allow the children to romp and play in the living room the next day.

The children's bedrooms should also be kept modestly clean and orderly. Children can be taught to make their beds neatly with their mother's help. It is also a blessing in working together, over and over again, helping the children to do a better job than the time before.

I did not allow our children to play or keep their toys in their bedrooms because I wanted them to play where I was working. When young children develop the habit of playing where Mother works, as they grow older they will not be content to go to their bedroom to play. Even though it takes longer for a mother to do her work, it is such a blessing to have the children where she can hear and join in the conversation. As the children play or "help" their mother, it affords ample time for discussion and questions that mothers are best suited to answer.

Another purpose for children to play in the kitchen is that we do not entertain our visitors in the bedroom so why should our children entertain their guests in the bedroom? There were times when our guests' children asked about playing in the bedroom, and I would kindly but firmly say "no." I am sure many unwholesome conversations and actions can be avoided when we consistently live by God's principles. Table games can be played on the kitchen table or children can learn to sit and listen to what the older ones are saying.

We must teach our children to be trustworthy. We must make sure they are worthy of trust before we send them out into an untrustworthy and dishonest society. It takes time and effort, and we cannot afford to allow our children to play by themselves, where Mother is not aware of what is going on. Since children are full of folly (Proverbs 22:15), they need constant care and guidance.

There is a thought afloat that "quality time is more important than quantity time" but this has not proven to be true! They are of equal importance. Many questions and ideas that make up the child cannot be related and shared in short order. Mothers must *be there* and listen. That way she knows what her children are thinking and can give proper guidance. It is at this age that open communication begins and good relationships are built that last a lifetime.

Our children developed an appreciation for an orderly bedroom. It was there that they slept rather than played; therefore, they found it frustrating when there was disorder. There is a great need today to instill a diligent and honest spirit in our children. Many times children are more content to help in their own way than to be told to run and play. I'm sure it takes longer to get things done when our children are underfoot, but what is the hurry? We are raising God's children for eternal purposes! Certainly it is important to get our work done and our house clean, but since our spiritual and material phase of life is so interwoven, we are what we are and that is what our children will become. Therefore, we must keep our priorities straight. The bathroom is another very important room to keep clean. Imagine living a hundred years ago, using outdoor facilities. Here we are with all the modern conveniences! Frequently these rooms are not kept as clean and sanitary as they could be. It does not take long to scrub the toilet often to prevent repulsive odors. Children need to be taught to use these facilities correctly. Little boys can be taught to "sink the boat" by putting a small piece of toilet tissue into the toilet for their aim. Children must be taught to wash their hands and flush the toilet, even if they must stand on the toilet seat or use a small step stool in order to reach the sink. Faucets can be marked to distinguish between hot and cold. Perhaps our first thought is "I don't have time," but it is these little areas that bring joy. Our work as mothers is not getting the work done ourselves but sharing the load. Through this, our children are taught responsibility.

Spring and fall housecleaning is another duty that can be viewed with dread. Perhaps you feel it is not needful, or maybe once a year is sufficient for you. One mother has a goal to clean thoroughly one room each month; for another, it's done whenever she feels like it; and even for another, she would rather rummage through crowded closets to find what she is looking for. Nevertheless, I find it is important to go through the whole house in the spring and fall. Since our wedding anniversary is the middle of March and my birthday is the middle of September, I have these dates as my goal to have my housecleaning completed. Usually during the month of February, I do the necessary painting or wallpaper hanging, clean out every nook and closet; then in the fall I go through it a bit more quickly.

For years I would try to prepare my family for these

"house-shaking" events because no one fancied the distuptions. One spring I decided I'd try another method. I quietly went through the rooms, cleaning one room at a time, being more careful not to upset too much at once. One day when I went to town to rent the steam vacuum, my husband son were so suprised; they hadn't even been aware of what I was doing. So after that success, I no longer tried to prepare them but quietly went about my work. I believe it was more joyful for all involved.

When we accept the role of homemaking, we accept many unknown events that will take place, such as cooking, cleaning, and perhaps many lowly, unnoticed tasks. In doing these, we are living in obedience to God because true faithfulness brings true joy and fulfillment.

Our senses must be sharp to be aware of what is going on around us. If we want to prevent mishaps, we must teach and train consistently day in and day out. Isaiah 28:10 reminds us it is "precept upon precept; line upon line." Deuteronomy 6:7,8 and Deuteronomy 11:19-21 reminds us of nearly the same message. There is never a vacation from teaching and training our children.

It is easy to fail to detect problems soon enough. We choose which we will be doing: either we'll be busy preventing errors, or we'll have a lot of repairing to do in broken relationships and communications. Good relationships bring joy and gladness to housecleaning. When we fail, we spend our latter years lamenting, "If only I had. . . ." Doing things God's way is being aware that an ounce of prevention is worth a pound of cure! When we truly love our children as God loves us, we will be deeply concerned about their spiritual well-being. Therefore, we will deal sternly with sin, keeping their good in mind.

It is of utmost importance to be aware that as we clean the house, we also need to check and cleanse our heart. Every thought and attitude must be pure and clean in order to have a blessed abode for our Lord and Saviour Jesus Christ. Just as we desire Jesus to be the center of our homes, so He must first dwell in our pure hearts. Jesus is really the key to a joyful life of housecleaning.

A Mother From A-Z

A *ttitudes of joy make her home a pleasant place to be.*

B *lessings are many as she balances the budget and plans for the family.*

C *heerfulness is her lot as she oversees her household tasks.*

D *uties, whether great or small, are all fulfilled by dilligence.*

E *nthusiasm marks her labor in the garden as she plans for the winter meals.*

F *aithfully she cans and freezes for the family and friends alike.*

G *ratitude is in her heart, even though she is weary to the bone.*

H *ealth is important to her, both physical and spiritual.*

I *ndustry provides a channel for her energies.*

J *ustice and mercy go hand in hand as she disciplines the children.*

K *nowledge of the scripture is her guide for life.*

L *ove, the greatest virtue, makes duty a delight.*

M *eekness describes her way; she is not proud or boastful.*

N *ever does she cease to pray and nurse her family.*

O *beys her Father; therefore, she commands obedience from her children.*

P *atiently she teaches, line upon line, here and there a little.*

Q *uietness and confidence in the Lord is her strength.*

R *ight living brings her life above reproach.*

S *inging lifts hers and the family's spirits; therefore, imparting blessings.*

T *rusting in the Lord is her motto.*

U *nderstanding is what she prays for daily.*

V *igilance is needed to keep her household in order.*

W *aiting on the Lord, she finds answers to the children's questions.*

'X *periences many joys as she mothers her children from total dependence to independence.*

Y *ields not to the temptation to compare herself with others.*

Z *ealous for the Lord by serving her family and others.*

Is this the description of you?

24

Retracing My Steps

I tiptoed down the hall. What a moment of quietness, of awesome relief, for both babies were asleep. How I longed for those quiet times, when I could be alone with God and sort out my priorities.

This illustrates the daily grind of life most young mothers face. Finding time to be alone with God is very difficult, because of urgent demands.

My desire was to grow in holiness and become better acquainted with God's holy Word. The only way to accomplish this, we usually decide, is to spend more time with God. But there is another aspect. The reality of becoming holy does not happen only as we read the Bible and pray; it happens in everyday life, as we by His strength and grace apply His Word and obediently act upon it.

As a very young, immature Christian in my early twenties, I found myself an overwhelmed mother of a tiny baby and a toddler. Knowing God was still my real concern, but how could I get to know Him better?

God always has a plan, even though He may not allow circumstances to change or adjustments and schedules to become lighter. He chose to use my babies as His instruments in changing my life. He taught me lessons that would help me progress toward growth.

God started where it hurt most—with self. Nothing hinders fellowship with God more than self-centeredness. I thought I had died to self, but motherhood was my proving ground.

Toddlers and babies have ways of being demanding. Consequently, I soon learned that selfishness must go or sanity will. Sacrifice becomes the way of a mother's life. I soon learned I must focus on others, not on self. Dying to self is not easy, but the rewards of freedom from self-centeredness make it well worth the effort.

Dying to self teaches many lessons, and one of them is servanthood. We must learn to orient our lives to meet the needs of others. For a mother, servanthood is an absolute necessity. Mothers do not have time to think, "Shall I serve or not?" They just serve!

There is no sleeping late mornings, no quiet evening to pursue a hobby, no reading for relaxation. Each day consists of feeding, bathing, cleaning up the house, caring for husband and children. By evening, sleep is often a welcome relief from a busy day.

Children are good teachers in endurance and patience. This does not consist of one day of hard work or one early morning rising, but rather years of interruptions and demands. I was forced to develop self-discipline and diligence. Day after day, it is the same routine, and often without recognition or reward. But the discipline and diligence I gained in the process are valued results.

Humility, too, is learned. Many times I failed in being patient and kind. By failing in these areas I failed God. Then to face God after such failures would only draw me to Him for strength, help, and wisdom.

Had I focused only on the moment, I possibly would have despaired. But, instead, as I labored I recognized this was my God-given lot in life, and each day I enjoyed His blessing through the lives of our children.

My desire to grow in Christ's likeness was granted and, too, God blessed me with a burden to also help the children grow to shoulder responsibility and to be aware of His requirements in obedience and respect.

When we have the proper perspective, we will use our possessions to build our children. We will not use our children to increase our possessions.

Then, too, in our concern to provide a pleasant atmosphere for our children, we need continually to remind ourselves that we dare not fail the Lord by failing our children. Nor do we want to fail our children by failing to keep God first in our priorities.

It helped me to remember that, as mothers, we are models that should recommend nothing to our children that we have not already tried and found to be what we feel is best.

One such example is in living a consistent, disciplined life. Through this, we teach the importance of endurance. We are not called to an easy life, but by God's grace to endure hardness (II Timothy 2:3).

Now here I am, retracing my steps after 27 years of mothering. Someone nobly said, "Once a mother, always a mother." My ears still catch those cries, "Mama, Mama!" Even though these cries call for other mothers, I'm still reminded of my struggles, failures, victories, joys and all the happiness little children bring.

My desire is to encourage and pray for young mothers as I observe them caring for their babies and children. There are times when I notice a mother who looks weary, one who needs to mete out discipline. Or I see a mother getting up from her chair numbers of times to make sure her orders are carried out. These mothers need all the encouragement they can get to be consistent.

Motherhood usually begins early in life, while one may still be an immature, floundering, young Christian. I am thankful God planned it that way. It is with a grateful heart that I observe our daughter-in-law. She consistently keeps her eyes on her young son and has her ears tuned to hear. At times it seems as if she has eyes in the back of her head; very few misdeeds escape her attention.

This is the way God planned it! God gives grace to be

consistent, even when Mother is tired, because her goal has far-reaching effects. As we do our best, we have the confidence that God will do the rest.

This, then, can be our prayer:

Build me children, O Lord, strong enough to face themselves when they are afraid. May they be honest and humble and gentle.

Build me children whose wishbone will not replace their backbone, children who know Thee. To know Thee as Lord and Saviour is the foundation of true knowledge and wisdom.

Lead them, I pray, not in paths of ease and comfort; but, under the stress and difficulties of life, spur them on by challenges. Here let them learn compassion for those who fail.

Build me children whose hearts are pure and clean, whose goals are high, children who master themselves by Your help; who learn to laugh, yet don't forget how to weep; who reach into the future; yet never ignore the past.

And after these things are theirs, I pray give them humility so that they may always remember the simplicity of true greatness, be open to true wisdom, and in meekness find true strength.

Then I, their mother, by Your grace may dare to whisper, "I have not lived in vain."

Excellence is not sinless perfection, but rather, a pure heart that desires to grow in Christ's likeness.

When I Have Time

When I have time, so many things I'll do
To make life happier and much more fair
For those who lives are crowded now with care.
I'll help to lift them from their low despair,
        When I have time.

When I have time, the friend I love so well
Shall know no more these weary toiling days:
I'll lead her feet in pleasant paths always,
And cheer her heart with words of sweetest praise,
        When I have time.

When you have time! The friend you hold so dear
May be beyond the reach of your intent;
May never know what you so kindly meant
To fill her life with love and sweet content,
        When you had time.

Now is the time! Ah, friend, no longer wait
To scatter loving smiles and words of cheer
To those around whose lives are now so drear,
They may not meet you in the coming year—
        Now is the time!

Courtesy of Sword of the Lord Publishers, Murfresboro, TN, 1969.
Used by permission.

25

Working Myself Out of a Job

A woman's life consists of continual change. Therefore, it is so important that we learn contentment. Paul's testimony in Philippians 4:11 is, "For I have learned, in whatsoever state I am, therewith to be content."

A woman does not enjoy stress, because stress takes its toll. First, she is a bride, learning the basics of relating to her husband. Then, she becomes a mother of small children, who need much care and attention. In the next phase, she finds herself involved in school lessons and school-related activities. Then, suddenly, she is aware that the children do not need that constant care they once demanded. She may feel threatened by her children's independence, but this should not be, and will not be, if she has the proper concept of life.

In this stage of life, she could make the mistake of believing she is no longer needed and withdraw into a shell of self-pity. But her children need her now more than ever; however, in a different way. Earlier, she instructed and they followed carefully. Her position now is to be available to listen, to encourage, and to lend a helping hand when needed. She must be there and be interested. Otherwise, she may lose the valuable art of communication with her family at a very crucial point. The teenager must know there is a praying mother who is interceding to God for her children, one who listens without lecturing or "preaching." It is within this phase of life that she comes to the stark realization that she is slowly working herself out of a constant job of mothering.

In order to face graciously the stress of many changes, she must have proper concept of short- and long-term goals. She must also find fulfillment and contentment because God is leading. Then the stress will not become overwhelming.

One real blessing is that God has wisely planned for husband and wife to parent their children and unitedly face the changes that are sure to come. Since their joy and fulfillment is not found in going places, in material possessions, or in circumstances, they become richer and more content as they follow Christ and grow up in Him. "That Christ may dwell in your hearts by faith; that ye, being rooted and grounded in love . . ." (Ephesians 3:17). This is the only way to accept changes and grow older cheerfully.

Mother and Father together must remember that whether their children spend eternity in heaven or hell, whether they rise to success or sink to failure, and whether they find fulfillment or live in confusion depends largely on their home training. The example of parents sets the stage for their children's well-being. What an awesome responsibility to accept that our children's security, the noblest issue in their lives, revolves around the center of parental interest. One of the greatest tragedies of this age is the unmistakable indifference on the part of parents toward this basic truth.

Parents must recognize that they are ordained by God to scrutinize the demands of this life in order to meet their children's spiritual and physical needs. If parents are preoccupied with business or social obligations, some of these should be dropped since the collapse of parental authority is one of the major factors in the staggering rise of delinquency. It is, therefore, imperative that God's plan for the family is followed closely and carefully. Every phase of life is ordered by God, and He has our good in mind. King Solomon gives us the key to victorious living. In Ecclesiastes 12, we are admonished to remember our Creator in our youth, before we become involved in so many things that draw our attention away from God. Hannah had a proper concept of working herself out of a job. She prayed for a son and God answered her prayer (I Samuel 1:27, 28). She promised to give him back to God all the days of his life. She recognized that God had only lent Samuel to her for a short time, to nurture and train for God's service.

Moses' parents are another example of diligent parenting that paid dividends. They had the privilege of leading their young son for several years before the king's daughter adopted him as her son. Hebrews 11:24-26 gives Moses' testimony. He chose to suffer affliction with God's people rather than to enjoy the temporary pleasures of Egypt. Moses kept the reward of heaven in view. He had a proper concept of life and eternity because his parents dared to instill principles into his young life. These principles developed into conviction that lasted all his life.

Mrs. Zebedee was a typical mother! She had high and noble goals for her two sons, James and John. Her encounter with Jesus is recorded in Matthew 20:20-22. She requested that her sons sit on Jesus' right and left in His kingdom. Perhaps we are too much like Mrs. Zebedee. We pray selfishly that our children fill some prominent position, or we encourage them to marry some popular individual rather than praying for God's will to be done and encouraging them to be faithful wherever God calls. Our responsibility is to teach by our life and example that Jesus deserves all our allegiance. Only as we die to self can our lives be blessed and fulfilled.

John the Baptist showed us by his example how to work ourselves out of a job. He was sent by God to prepare the way for Jesus. John said, "He must increase, but I must decrease" (John 3:30). As we see our children grow in their Christian life and develop convictions in the wisdom and knowledge of God, we must step aside gradually and allow them to become personally responsible and accountable to God. Again, we find that the constant job of parenting is lessening as the children grow up. Never, though, do we arrive at a plateau that releases us from the responsibility of encouragement, counsel, prayer, and intercession for them. Like Job we must pray and ask God's continual blessing and protection and forgiveness upon them (Job 1:5).

Through every phase of life, women must nourish their souls with good works. They can find joy and peace in solitude, find strength in prayer, and become wise by reading God's Word. We must always seek to reflect God's radiance even in our busy lives. Perhaps someone asks, "Who has time for all this?" Our older years will be only as rich and joyful and fulfilling as we make the day, today! We usually find time to do the things we want to do most. Why else do we have all these laborsaving devices in our homes? Often we fail to realize that we will be forever what we are becoming today. Instead of taking time to do what we should, we say, "Someday things will be different. Someday I'll have more time. Sometime when the children are grown, I'll do this or that."

Years ago I observed a certain older sister who was a good example for me as a young mother. Her dedication to God and her family was outstanding. She had a large family and enjoyed each. Later, in their forties, God blessed them with two more children. All too soon, these two grew up and left home. As she was going through this stage in life, I noticed she no longer seemed to be the joyful mother she had been; instead, stress and a nervous state took its toll.

As mothers, we need to keep in mind that life does continually change. It is very needful to plan for our future, even while our days do not contain enough hours to get the things done that need our attention. We must keep in mind that we are really working ourselves out of the job of mothering. Therefore, it is imperative to plan, or at least pray, and be open to prepare for when we are older and life is less demanding. It is important to have some other interest through which we can find fulfillment in years to come. Some find real fulfillment in returning to the classroom as a teacher. Some enjoy being more involved in voluntary work in the church or community. Others have returned to their former career of nursing. Some need to spend more time with their elderly parents. There is a great need for writing and artist work for our church papers. Many avenues are opened for the Christian woman who has been faithful within the four walls of her home. I keep reminding myself that we must always have time for our husbands, children, and grandchildren. When we seek God's will in areas such as this, God has promised we shall find His plan and His blessing even in this stage of life.

Some time ago, a friend of mine shared that an older friend encouraged her and her husband to leave the needs at home and in the church saying, "You need to enjoy yourself and relax. You need to get away. You owe it to yourself." The wise man, Solomon, has good counsel for this older friend. "Vanity of vanities, saith the Preacher, vanity of vanities; all is vanity. What profit hath a [woman] of all [her] labour which [she] taketh under the sun?" (Ecclesiastes 1:2, 3). In the following verses (4-8), he describes a life that characterizes "going in circles." "One generation passeth away, and another generation cometh. . . . The sun also riseth and goeth down. . . . The wind goeth toward the south, and turneth about unto the north; it whirleth about continually . . . the wind returneth . . . to his circuits. . . . the eye is not satisfied with seeing, nor the ear filled with hearing." King Solomon allowed his selfish nature to dictate his life. Therefore, he was not fulfilled, but rather empty, because he went in circles. The carnal person is never satisfied; he always craves something new, something exciting and more thrilling. King Solomon experienced everything his heart desired, and in his older age he confessed it to be vanity of vanities and even vexation of spirit. It is no wonder, that twelve chapters later, Solomon pleads that all people *remember now their creator* in their youth (Ecclesiastes 12:1). My friend was frustrated. She did not feel she needed to "get away." She loved and was concerned about her family and also the well-being of the church. She was a good example of a mother who was finding joy and fulfillment right at home. In order to do so, we must continually live by Proverbs 3:5, 6: "Trust in the Lord with *all* thy heart, and lean not unto thine own understanding. In all thy ways acknowledge him, and he shall direct thy paths" (italics added). We dare not allow the world in which we live to dictate our thinking or make us discontent with God's many blessings in the Christian family.

If we expect our older age to be a blessing, we must be found living for God *now*. We should not wait until our hair turns gray, then try to quickly become what God desires. We must be found in God's righteousness today, so that God can bless our latter years as well. "The hoary head is a crown of glory, if it be found in the way of righteousness" (Proverbs 16:31).

Job 5:26 compares growing older to a ripened shock of grain. Age is inevitable, yet God leaves the choice with each person as to whether we will grow older cheerfully and joyfully, or whether we will try to deny our age. For the Christian woman, it is a blessing to realize God has so graciously led her safely thus far, and by His grace she will continue to enjoy living in the realm God has so wisely designed for her.

Life can also be likened to fruit trees. Every year, the grower expects more and better fruit. So it is with God: every year He expects His children to yield more and richer fruit. Like the grower, God patiently cares for us and permits joys and sorrows to make us more refined and mature. If we view aging from a human perspective, we will be discontent and complaining. Psalm 90:12 tells us to number our days, not our years. We must live one day at a time. As we live by His principles, He will provide daily strength and grace to live enthusiastically for Him. If we accept each day as a gift from God, we will be controlled by His grace to live for His glory.

Is growing older dreadful? Never.
Challenging? Yes.
Changing? Often.
Humbling? Occasionally.
Rewarding? Eternally.

But the key to living realistically is:
to give graciously,
adapt willingly,
trust fearlessly,
rejoice daily.

"So the Lord blessed the latter end of Job more than his beginning" (Job 42:12a). It is God's perfect will that we enjoy each day that has been allotted to us. By God's grace, our latter end, like Job's, can also be more blessed.

Looking for the Sunrise

I'm not looking for the sunset
    As the swift years come and go;
I am looking for the sunrise
    And the golden morning glow,
Where the light of heaven's glory
    Will break forth upon my sight,
In the land that knows no sunset
    Nor the darkness of the night.

I'm not going down the pathway
    Toward the setting of the sun,
Where the shadows ever deepen
    When the day at last is done;
I am walking up the hillside,
    Where the sunshine lights the way
To the glory of the sunrise
    Of God's never-ending day.

I'm not going down, but upward,
    And the path is never dim,
For the day grows ever brighter
    As I journey on with Him.
So my eyes are on the hilltops,
    Waiting for the sun to rise—
Waiting for the invitation
    To the home beyond the skies.

—Author unknown

TO ORDER

For additional copies send $6.95
(plus $2.00 postage and handling)
to:
Calvary Publications
The Bylers
Rt. 1, Box 630
Stuarts Draft, Virginia 24477

Quantity discounts available.

Name _____

Address _____

City _____ State _____ Zip _____

Quantity ordered _____

Amount enclosed _____

Virginia residents please include 4.5% sales tax.

TO ORDER

For additional copies send $6.95
(plus $2.00 postage and handling)
to:
Calvary Publications
The Bylers
Rt. 1, Box 630
Stuarts Draft, Virginia 24477

Quantity discounts available.

Name _____

Address _____

City _____ State _____ Zip _____

Quantity ordered _____

Amount enclosed _____

Virginia residents please include 4.5% sales tax.

TO ORDER

For additional copies send $6.95
(plus $2.00 postage and handling)
to:
Calvary Publications
The Bylers
Rt. 1, Box 630
Stuarts Draft, Virginia 24477

Quantity discounts available.

Name _____

Address _____

City _____ State _____ Zip _____

Quantity ordered _____

Amount enclosed _____

Virginia residents please include 4.5% sales tax.

Notes

Notes

Notes

Notes